Lara Croft

Lara Croft

Cyber Heroine

Astrid Deuber-Mankowsky

Translated by Dominic J. Bonfiglio
Foreword by Sue-Ellen Case

Electronic Mediations, Volume 14

University of Minnesota Press • Minneapolis • London

Published by the University of Minnesota Press
111 Third Avenue South, Suite 290
Minneapolis, MN 55401-2520
http://www.upress.umn.edu

Library of Congress Cataloging-in-Publication Data

Deuber-Mankowsky, Astrid, 1957–
  [Lara Croft. English]
  Lara Croft : cyber heroine / Astrid Deuber-Mankowsky ; translated by Dominic J. Bonfiglio ; foreword by Sue-Ellen Case.
    p. cm. — (Electronic mediations ; v. 14)
  Includes bibliographical references and index.
  ISBN 0-8166-4390-3 (hc : alk. paper) — ISBN 0-8166-4391-1 (pb : alk. paper)
  1. Croft, Lara (Fictitious character) in mass media. I. Title. II. Series.
  P96.C77D4813 2005
  793.93′2—dc22

2004027422

Contents

Foreword

Sue-Ellen Case

The character Lara Croft has become an icon, in the broadest sense of the word, for the female agent in the world of cyberspace. Lara originated in the popular computer game *Tomb Raider*, but she has extended her realm to twenty-one video games operating on six different systems (including a forthcoming mobile phone game), a line of Lara Croft action figures, two major movies, forty comic books, and a series of novels based on the video games. She has appeared on the covers of *Time* and *Newsweek* and inspired a beauty pageant designed to elect her corporeal representative. A Google search for Lara Croft online yields more than 2,140,000 results. Lara Croft fan sites are found most often in French, German, and Dutch, but she is also inscribed in Portuguese, Spanish, Czech, Russian, and Italian. Many fan sites perform fantasies of Lara, including fan fiction and photographs of users posing as Lara. Yet of those sites dedicated to Lara, 177,000 link the name Lara Croft with pornography. Her image thus organizes the interface between the representational status of women and the emerging discourse of interactive virtuality. A figure of empowerment, oscillating between subject and object, she excites identificatory and masturbatory fantasies. Like no other cyber-character, she marks success through a hypergendered muscular body trained to succeed in violent competition.

In spite of Lara's powerful iconicity, both for the realm of the cyber and for the use of the image of woman in that realm, few critical or historical treatments of this phenomenon have appeared, either online or in hard copy. This new translation of Astrid Deuber-Mankowsky's *Lara Croft* provides a much-needed critical treatment of this powerful, influential fantasy that has focused the identificatory needs of an entire generation obsessed with digital representations. Moreover, it is important to translate this book into English, for as much as Lara Croft may be an international celebrity, she is a specifically American production, produced by and producing the necessary requirements for cultural and digital imperialism.

Deuber-Mankowsky's book is a pioneering effort to conjoin feminist theory with new media studies. She provides a matrix of critiques and interpretations of the cyber, as earlier books such as Teresa de Lauretis's *Alice Doesn't* provided for film studies. In fact, Deuber-Mankowsky brings the critical conjunction of gender theory, theories of representation, and the gendering of the apparatus from earlier studies of feminist film theory to bear on the new media. Obviously, while the digital modes of production and reception share some common strategies with film, they operate quite differently from film. Deuber-Mankowsky thus invents an original critical paradigm for the function of the sign of woman in relation to the hardware and software of its production. In the way that earlier feminist theory offered the new paradigm of the male gaze and installed it in seemingly value-free machines such as the camera, Deuber-Mankowsky marks computer and software production with the social practices of masculinity.

The book begins by establishing a historical ground for its critical strategies, carefully plotting the development of the game and the computer platform that supported it, as well as its market success. Lara appears as a figure of successful graphics development. At the same time, she operates as the figural magnet for commercial tie-ins, linking games with movies, toys, Web sites, and so on. A new type of icon emerges, composed of character, logo, and celebrity. As Deuber-Mankowsky notes, William Gibson's novel *Idoru* fully imagines how this new form of synthetic "star" may appear, with a new version of success and profit. Unlike Gibson's portrayal, this book reveals how it is specifically through uses of the image of a woman that this market and industrial prowess could successfully interface with its users.

Part of Lara's success depends on the content of her image. Of course, her lineage of whiteness and class privilege provides a certain allure. She is also an independent woman, working in "other" countries as an archaeologist. Deuber-Mankowsky rehearses the various possibilities for identification offered by the content of the image and its narrative, outlining both the positive and negative aspects of its referents. On the one hand, Lara represents a strong, independent woman, available to young girls as a role model. In fact, there is evidence that her image has inspired some young women to desire to become archaeologists. On the other hand, she functions as the sexualized object of the gaze. In the porn sites, her most pronounced characteristic is her ample breasts: the visible markers of sexual seduction. Other critical treatments of Lara Croft provide a similar analysis of the relation of this content to user, much as early feminist studies identified the roles women are made to play, such as wife, mother, virgin, whore, and so forth. But in this book the referents of the image compose the ground for its critical argument, rather than its conclusion, and here is where it makes a major contribution to the field. *Lara Croft* participates in the feminist critique of mimesis, from Luce Irigaray's *Speculum* to Elin Diamond's *Unmaking Mimesis*. It seeks to create a philosophical critique of the operating structures of mimesis rather than of their referents. Historically specific and materially grounded, structures of mimesis embed the ontological and material ideologies of the cultures deploying the dynamics of imitation. In the world of new media studies, this has been phrased as "the medium is the message," and Marshall McLuhan does make an appearance in the text. But how does one decode the message "Lara Croft" when, as Deuber-Mankowsky puts it, she is more about data structures than narratives?

More than a woman archaeologist, then, in this book Lara Croft is treated as a fetish in the medium of advanced capitalist circulation. She animates the mediatized body as a capitalized zone for binding the binary codes of gender, sexual difference, and heterosexuality with the binaries of the real and the virtual realms. This is a complex argument, engaging with a wide variety of feminist concerns. First, the very nature of the virtual is interrogated, as it emerges not from photographic representation but from data structures. Then the semiotic function of Lara's image is reconfigured within the digital field and interactive environment. Does something like the notion of the gaze, so central to feminist film theory, operate within the environment of new media? Deuber-Mankowsky argues that Lara animates the data, like a dream, both performing and displacing the memory of the machine. Yet how does the interactive user participate in this production? These are questions central to studies of new media, often posed with no sense that gender plays a central role in the process. Deuber-Mankowsky injects them with the full feminist critique.

As the book proceeds, Lara's accumulation of semiotic functions leads to the signature tropes of computer games, such as violence and death. The narratives of violence and death, in the virtual realm, are perceived as disavowing their own results. Rather than invoking narrative endings, these tropes are revealed as actually bolstering a masculinized version of digital transcendence. It is important to note that the notion of a masculinized investment in digital transcendence has also appeared in the works of Katherine Hayles and Vivian Sobchack, lending an amplification to this strategy across fields. And yet Lara Croft, while figuring this transcendence, also descends from her virtual heights to become corporealized through the bodies of "real" women. What does it mean to invert the traditional relations of mimesis, making real life a mirror of art? The corporeal imitation of the virtual? How does the concept of the body, so central to feminist studies, function in this inversion? To engage with these conundrums, Deuber-Mankowsky moves to psychoanalytic considerations of desire vis-à-vis surface and illusion.

I have tried to illustrate the many uses of this book for readers of feminist theory and those who study new media. By invoking the icon of Lara Croft, Deuber-Mankowsky has established a focus for this intersection of fields, providing the kind of theoretical leadership in the new media that feminism has so crucially offered in film and performance.

The Phenomenon of Lara Croft

"Lara, your name says a thousand words."

So begins a fan letter to Lara Croft. It is one of many that can be found on the Internet. Of those thousand words the name Lara is supposed to say, the letter's author has found ninety-five. He uses them to compose a love poem, one whose first lines give a vivid impression of what could be called "the phenomenon of Lara Croft":

> Luscious, Likeable, Lovely, Loving, and Loved. Lonely
> sometimes? A Landmark in computer game history. You
> speak everyone's Language, a top Lass. You Leap, Lean,
> and Look, Leaving nothing but empty tombs. Daughter
> of Lord Henshingley Croft. Adventurous, Adaptable to
> any surroundings, and Anatomically perfect. An
> Achiever, Accurate (You never miss!) and heavily
> Acclaimed by all.[1]

Lara stands for a thousand names, for just as many desires and hopes. Her fans have loved her as they would a star. Indeed, they have loved her more than they would a star, for experiencing Lara in the video game makes possible an intimacy unequaled by the public appearances of music, film, and television celebrities. Lara is not only the beloved; she is also the lover. Yet how can a lover emerge from what my then-fourteen-year-old son described as "pixel porridge"?[2]

In the beginning, Lara Croft was a video game figure like many others. The only things distinguishing the main character of *Tomb Raider* from those of other video games were her sex and improved graphics. Yet soon after its release in November 1996, *Tomb Raider* sales were among the highest on the game market, and Lara Croft gained global fame. She was the first virtual figure to make the transition from the game world into universal media reality. Just months after the game appeared on the market, Lara Croft could be seen on billboards, on television, on magazine covers, in leading game journals, and in various daily newspapers and weekly publications. Young women lent Lara Croft their bodies as her official representatives in the real world, giving interviews and autographs on Lara's behalf and letting themselves be photographed in her trademark attire. Lara appeared at rock concerts, served as a model for fashion designers, and promoted products ranging from watches and cars to soft drinks and newspapers. Matching her ubiquity in conventional media was her popularity on the Internet. From June 1997 to May 2002, the *Croft Times,* an online newspaper appearing in several different languages, regularly reported on the Lara cosmos. Thousands of fan sites, online magazines, and chat rooms kept track of her every move. Lara's transmedial presence ultimately earned her the title of "cultural icon" for the new media society.

Along with a presence across different media, the phenomenon of Lara Croft brought with it the ability to mediate among them. Rumors about a planned Hollywood movie started to circulate as early as 1997. In the winter of 1998, Paramount Pictures announced that it had purchased the film rights to *Tomb Raider* and planned to make a multi-hundred-million-dollar trilogy. In the spring of 2000, it was made known that the Oscar-winning actress Angelina Jolie would play the part of Lara Croft. The virtual star was now to be embodied by a real one. When shooting started in August of that year, minute details of the movie's progress were regularly posted on the Internet. The first previews could be downloaded that fall.

What kept this media fever going? What kinds of mechanisms, what kinds of contingencies, what kinds of forces combined to turn a more or less wooden game figure with rudimentary facial expressions into a dream woman and cultural icon?

My work on Lara Croft began in the summer of 1999 during a seminar I held at the Institute for Cultural Studies at Humboldt University in Berlin entitled "Femininity, Representation, and Gender." Lara Croft was one of the subjects we examined while discussing various theories of representation and representation critique. At the time, *Tomb Raider III* was hitting record sales on the global video game market. The German *Lara Croft Magazin* had just appeared, and its first issue featured Lara wearing custom-designed fashions, including a bikini by Gucci.[3] Six months earlier, in a talk at the Social Market Foundation, the British science minister, Lord Sainsbury of Turville, had suggested using Lara Croft as an ambassador for British scientific excellence. According to Sainsbury, Lara Croft was living proof that the United Kingdom stood at the cutting edge of new developments.[4] Around the same time, a columnist for a conservative feminist online publication named Lara as her pick for

Republican candidate in the 2000 presidential election.[5] A "Lara for President" campaign subsequently made its way through the media. Later that summer, *Playboy* published nude pictures of a former Lara Croft model for its August 1999 issue. Just as the magazine was being released in the United Kingdom, Core Design, Lara Croft's creator, obtained a court injunction preventing *Playboy* from printing the Lara Croft name and *Tomb Raider* logo alongside the pictures.[6] The company's lawyer claimed that the association with the magazine would tarnish the image of the fictional star. The court ordered *Playboy* to apply stickers blanking out any reference to Lara Croft or *Tomb Raider* on the covers of magazines yet to be distributed.

Instead of offering satisfying answers, my initial attempts at explaining the phenomenon of Lara Croft only raised more and more questions. My search first led me to the economic and political conditions of the computer and video game market. I began to investigate the significance of technical innovations for game success and development, especially in the area of graphics, and examined the relationship between software and hardware, PC and console. In their interactions, these aspects proved to have their own inherent codes and principles, ones that determine not only a game's story line but also its protagonists. In addition, I discovered that links to other media, particularly those to Hollywood cinema and its star industry, played a key role in producing the phenomenon of Lara Croft. Yet all of these together could not explain Lara's particular success. Instead it became progressively clear that filling the explanatory gap would entail directing my attention to the changes to which new media subject our bodily perception and desire. In pursuing these changes, I was led back to the concept of sexual difference. From here the questions guiding my thinking on Lara Croft emerged:

How can analyzing the phenomenon of Lara Croft help us better understand the shifts in meaning currently taking place in the concepts of gender, sex, and sexuality?

Has Lara Croft, at once pinup model and rebellious, man-repelling grrl, overstepped the boundaries between the sexes just as she has those between virtuality and reality?

A Duplicitous Gift

The problem that Lara Croft poses for feminist theory results from precisely those multiple meanings we saw celebrated in the opening line of her admirer's poem: through them Lara has been able to span the gap between men's sexual fantasies and women's longings for supernatural agility. More than merely an object of male desire, Lara Croft became the first positive female role model on the computer game market. She opened up the virtual game world to a whole generation of young women and girls.

The appearance of a heroine in a visual world with so few prompted an editor of a leading German feminist magazine to declare Lara Croft a gift of such importance that women have no choice but to accept her "oversize feminine attributes" as a "necessary tribute to the male world."[1] And indeed, Lara does more than fulfill men's fantasies with her "oversize feminine attributes" (i.e., those preternaturally large breasts whose origins and alteration have their own narrative in the Lara Croft universe). Women, especially girls, enjoy following the tough adventurer. In her, as many will admit, they feel represented as a woman—a woman who is independent, eager to live life to its fullest, one who is liberated and feels superior to men.

Fostering this image is Lara Croft's biography. Eidos, the multinational corporation responsible for marketing *Tomb Raider,* provided Lara Croft with a blood type (AB–), hobbies (shooting and free climbing), a date of birth (February 14, 1968), parents, an education (private schools in England and Switzerland), a nationality (British), as well as her own childhood. The daughter of the British Lord Henshingley, Lara—so her invented biography goes—grew up in the secure world of the aristocracy, where she received a first-rate education and intensive athletic training. Were it up to her parents, Lara would have married early and started a family befitting her social standing. But a decisive turn of events changes Lara's life. An airplane crash in the Himalayas leaves Lara the only survivor, and she must make her way alone through the mountains for two weeks. It is an experience that puts Lara on the path of becoming the adventurer and tomb raider we know from the computer game: a woman hungry for life, craving freedom and travel, a woman who is independent, self-confident, beautiful, and always taking new risks.[2]

Yet a closer look at this purported gift will show it to be a duplicitous one, for beyond being the object of male and female desire, Lara Croft governs over a hierarchical order of the sexes replete with all the gender stereotypes that feminist theory has been decoding and deconstructing for more than thirty years. Although Lara Croft promotes a process that can be described as at once degendering and medializing the body, this process does not surmount traditional prejudices but reverts to a heterosexual metaphysics of gender. Here we are presented with the paradoxical fact that the leveling of sexual difference and the consolidation of a dualistic order of the sexes are not mutually exclusive. Rather, in a way that is baffling yet logically consistent, each reinforces the other.

The problem with which the phenomenon of Lara Croft confronts us makes one thing clear: if feminist theory is to tackle the difficulties arising from the union of the old media with the new, methodological-critical reflection will be needed. In the face of a universal media society, the field of gender studies is called on to go beyond its traditional boundaries and borrow from the approaches of media theory.

So, for instance, however much Lara Croft serves male and female fantasies of power, she also, in the same breath, transforms all players into gender-neutral "users."[3] That is to say, male and female players are equally bound to the hardware through their desires and fantasies. The sexuality of the user plays a role only insofar as desire is directed toward the medium; once the player begins using the PC or game console, his or her sexuality becomes unimportant. Lara Croft's ability to attract men and women merely satisfies the simple demand that the circle of users increase—a demand she meets with proven artistry. The secret of her appeal to both sexes lies, as the admirer wrote in his fan letter, in her ability to speak "everyone's language." Lara Croft's message awakens the desire of both men and women alike.

Following recent German theorists, I understand media to include "all those material technologies and common forms distributed throughout society whose application determines the collective configuration of perception and experience in our world."[4] Important here is the impact that the technical and material side of media has on perception and communication. The computer is not only a machine or tool; it is also a medium that determines *how* we perceive just as much as *what* we perceive.[5] Any notion of media that remains exclusively oriented to technical aspects cannot sufficiently explain the interaction between the "new media" and their users. We must also consider the concept of the medium from the other side, as it were—from the position of the user.

From this vantage point, we can see that every medium is part of a "sign-event," one that is accompanied by what Slavoj Žižek aptly describes as "the emergence of the pure appearance which cannot be reduced to the simple effect of its bodily causes."[6] That even the technical definition of a computer relies on a nonmaterial sign-event is shown by the expression "virtual machine." By inventing this new terminology, computer scientists wanted to account for the fact that the majority of today's users see the machine component of the computer through the programs of the operating system, while what really happens in the hardware is known only by the engineers.[7] In determining hardware function, the operating system mediates between user program and machine.[8] The computer is, in other words, a medium in the form of a virtual machine, a machine that is accessible only by means of software, that is, signs. It is a medium without a gender, one for which the sexuality of its users is irrelevant.

Lara Croft is a different kind of medium entirely. She speaks everyone's language and her name says, as her fan formulated so well, a thousand words. This makes her into a universal medium of circulation, one that, unlike machines and operating systems, is entitled to a gender. The medium represented by Lara Croft is universal and feminine. The effect of a sign-event, she invites the user to interact with the computer in such a way that the user completely forgets the reality of the machine whose virtualization has already been prepared by the software interposed between user and hardware. As I will argue in more detail, the medium of Lara Croft was not conceived as feminine by accident. The connotations of mediality, representation, and femininity follow a long tradition, one that recurs in the establishment of new media. To analyze the phenomenon of Lara Croft, we will have to look into the question of how the linking of these two media—virtual machine and Lara Croft—came about and what ramifications it has had.

Adhering to the same logic described by Karl Marx in his chapter on the commodity fetish in *Capital*, Lara Croft, like money itself, functions as a medium of circulation erasing all qualitative difference, even sexual difference.[9] To better characterize this medialization of the body, I would first like to distance the concept of sexual difference from any associations it might have with an identity-fixated heterosexuality based solely on gender. Following Judith Butler, I understand sexual difference as an irresolvable question, not a scientific or philosophical object among many, but a place of unrest revealing the limits of epistemological validity.[10] The question of sexual difference aims to interrogate the historical basis of our knowledge and the unquestioned metaphysics of gender it presupposes. According to this metaphysics, the feminine is linked to the body, nature, matter, heteronomy, passivity, and the image, while the masculine is associated with thought (or mind), culture, form, autonomy, activity, and the gaze. The question of sexual difference, beyond its opposition to a gender-based dualism, is concerned with the connections that exist between gender identity, the play with truth, and the foundations of knowledge. The goal is not to define sexual difference better or more precisely, as was once the case, but to maintain it as a place of unrest—a gap through which, as the French philosopher Geneviève Fraisse writes, historicity enters into thought.[11] Sexual difference is not only an irresolvable question, but it also confronts thought itself with its own irresolvability. It cannot, therefore, be subsumed under the well-known and often-criticized distinctions between nature and culture, body and mind.[12] The implications of understanding sexual difference as an irresolvable question for the analysis of Lara Croft will become clear in the course of this book. At this point, I want to stress that the medialization and degendering of the body rewrite the very openness of sexual difference as a hierarchical gender dualism on the abstract level of the binary code. The linkage of these apparently opposing processes testifies to the complexity of the phenomenon of Lara Croft.

Allucquère Rosanne Stone has stressed that the process of degendering that accompanies the virtualization of reality, along with its flip side, the becoming real of virtuality, concerns all users, not just women. As Stone also makes quite clear, it is not a process to be welcomed. While considering what happens to the body when spaces of fantasy are linked globally through the Internet, she points out that "much of the work of cyberspace researchers . . . assumes that the human body is 'meat'— obsolete, as soon as consciousness itself can be uploaded into the network."[13] Separated from wishes, from the intellectual fantasy, even from its own desire, the body is imagined as a piece of dead flesh excluded from the reality of cyberspace. In contrast to the views of many cyberspace researchers, Stone emphasizes that the virtual community has no less a vulnerable origin in the mortal and sexual body, a body that is open to injury, a body that is constituted by a completely different kind of flesh than that which can be subsumed under the category of "meat." With this in mind, Stone writes, "No refigured virtual body, no matter how beautiful, will slow the death of a cyberpunk with AIDS."[14]

3

The Origins of a Cultural Icon

omb Raider is a so-called action-adventure game, which concentrates on the player's skill and quick reflexes. Lara Croft must hop and jump her way through dimly lit chambers, abandoned tombs, and old palaces located throughout the world in search of archaeological treasures and other valuable artifacts. During her adventures she encounters all different types of adversaries. In London she is up against punks, in the South Pacific she battles the natives, in Antarctica she must fight against opponents masked as seals. In other instances she contends with haunted statues or hostile monkeys. Along the way she must solve riddles of varying difficulty.

Lara Croft's immediate predecessor was Rick Dangerous, a rotund little man who wore a slouch hat and carried a pistol. Although his inventor claimed that Rick Dangerous was modeled after Indiana Jones, his appearance was closer to that of Super Mario. Rick Dangerous was the hero and namesake of the 1989 best-selling game launched by the small British software developer Core Design.

In 1996 Core released the first version of *Tomb Raider*. Its gameplay was almost identical to that of its predecessor. *Lara Croft Magazin* wrote that *Rick Dangerous* "could easily have passed under the name 'Tomb Raider.'"[1] What had changed were the graphics and the sex of the main character. The flat, two-dimensional environment of *Rick Dangerous,* constantly interrupted through scene and page breaks, was made into a continuous and complete 3-D world. From the rotund little figure of dangerous Rick emerged a comparatively tough yet tender woman. By 1998 this three-dimensional female Indiana Jones had transformed herself into the cultural icon known as Lara Croft.

Lara Croft is not only a symbol for a society turned *media* society. She also represents the medium in which the various other media transversally communicate with one another. This medial copulation links the media and the separate communities established around them, often not aware of each other's existence, into a quasi-integrated media society. One of the reasons for the success of Lara Croft is the "magic" she possesses as universal medium. She has brought together the press, television, radio, fashion, pop music, comics, computer games, cinema, advertising, dance,[2] and, above all, the Internet. As a symbol for mediality, Lara Croft is also a medium of circulation reducing the media and the public spheres they constitute to a common denominator.

So, for instance, television viewers who saw a commercial with Lara Croft could feel informed without ever having come close to the game. Such viewers would have had no difficulty discussing Lara Croft during an entertaining evening with friends. They could have talked about the billboards, the front pages of popular magazines, the scandal that broke out when hackers released a nonauthorized version of *Tomb Raider* featuring a naked Lara. Other topics could have included the game's record sales or a life-size Lara Croft figure seen at the department store. Talking about Lara Croft signaled that one belonged, that is to say, that one *also* belonged, to the new media society. These mutual assurances of belonging took place everywhere: during breaks at school, small talk at the workplace, telephone calls, conversations between grandmother and grandson—any place where talking about Lara Croft, regardless of the media used, signified living in one and the same world.

Lara Croft's unanticipated success as universal medium was also an obvious and priceless gift for Core Design. Even as Lara was endorsing products for companies such as Nike, she was also giving out free promotion for the game. Jeremy Heath-Smith, Core Design's founder, comments: "Who knows how many millions and millions of pounds' worth of free marketing we got from the press, by them putting it in front of people who'd then think, 'Well, wow, that looks like a great game.'"[3]

How can we explain Lara Croft's transformation from Rick Dangerous successor to multi-million-dollar advertising commodity, from action-adventure game figure to universal medium and cultural icon? I would like to argue that this transformation has three origins, each distinct yet overlapping, interrelating, and, as a result, mutually reinforcing. The first is economic in nature, the second medial, and the third sexual. I would like to pursue these three origins—origins that are also grounds—in order to describe the phenomenon of Lara Croft more exactly and investigate the conditions under which a medium can function as a cultural icon in the current media society. In all three of these origins, moreover, aspects of hardware and software development play a crucial role. Without them, neither Lara Croft nor her origins would be conceivable.

④

The Market and the Hardware

ore Design started out in 1988 as a small studio in Derby, England, specializing in the development of technologically advanced computer and video games. In the beginning, the company was run by Jeremy Heath-Smith and his brother, Adrian Smith, along with a handful of employees. By the end of 2000, Core Design had increased its staff to ninety and become a subsidiary of the multinational corporation Eidos, which took over the sales and marketing of Core's products.

In the early days, when Heath-Smith himself was still in charge of sales, the game market was being greatly transformed by the introduction of the Sega and Nintendo video game consoles. Heath-Smith cultivated a close relationship with Sega, and after the introduction of its Mega CD (the first CD-based console), Core Design developed the game *Thunderhawk* for the Sega system. Although the game was a success, the Mega CD was soon outdated. Only months after it appeared on the market, the hardware was, as Smith put it in an interview, "dead."[1] The failure of the Mega CD put Nintendo and its hero Super Mario in the lead.

Smith, when asked in the same interview about life before Lara, emphasized the importance of market factors for both game development and the genesis of Lara Croft:

> Before Lara? Back then the game industry had to
> struggle with far too many computer and console
> variants. That meant that we had to program more
> games. Core was simultaneously developing software
> for Amiga, Atari ST, PC, and the Mega Drive.[2]

The appearance of Lara, Smith continued, coincided with the breakthrough of 32-bit platforms: "From that point on, everything was different." The significantly greater performance of 32-bit systems—they operated at speeds five hundred times faster than 16-bit platforms—revolutionized game design and became decisive in competition among hardware manufacturers. Sony was the first to introduce a 32-bit system in 1994. Its now legendary PlayStation dominated the market and put various other 16-bit consoles out of the running. Not until 1996, when Nintendo introduced its N64 console, did Sony have any competition. To give a sense of the economic ramifications of Sony's lead, the sales of PlayStation and its successor, PlayStation 2, are currently greater than sales of any other Sony product. By the end of 2000, over 80 million PlayStations had been sold.

Because of their improved graphics, 32-bit platforms could produce games whose appearance approached that of movies. This development toward "real-life" graphics was also shaped by another pivotal event: the introduction of 3-D graphics cards for the PC. With its ability to create explorable three-dimensional spaces on the computer screen, the PC was an ideal platform for games with advanced graphics and thus became a real contender on the video game market. Although consoles were more comfortable to use, PC graphics were far superior (and would remain so until the release of PlayStation 2.) It was now possible to design games for the PC that truly appeared movielike. This "incorporation" of the film medium, of course, anticipates Lara Croft's medial origins.

In 1995 Core Design developed its first game for the Sony PlayStation, *Thunderhawk 2*. In early 1996 Eidos took over Core Design, and at the end of the year, *Tomb Raider* appeared on the market. By that point, two decisive courses had already been set:

1. The first round of competition on the hardware market was decided, with the Sony PlayStation emerging as the apparent victor among 32-bit consoles. What's more, the introduction of 3-D graphics cards made computers perfect hardware for video games. The PlayStation's real competitor had become the PC.

2. The acquisition of Core Design by Eidos put the marketing of the software company's games into the hands of a multinational corporation. First off, this meant a separation of marketing and development. While the people at Core Design saw Lara Croft as a game hero in the tradition of Rick Dangerous, those at Eidos saw her primarily as an advertising figure. (As I will later argue in more detail, this was to make for an important difference.) The multi-nationality of the Eidos corporation ensured that games could be launched simultaneously throughout the world with the support of international advertising campaigns.

In an extremely clever move, Core Design developed three different versions of *Tomb Raider* concurrently, one for the PC, one for PlayStation, and one for Sega Saturn. In this way, the software could overcome the gaps that had opened up on the hardware market between PC and console-based systems. Core Design tapped the markets of each, mediating between the computer and video game communities.

In many respects Lara Croft had a global presence from the beginning. Eidos provided international distribution, while *Tomb Raider*'s compatibility with the two dominant hardware systems on the game market ensured medial presence on computer and television screens. Adding to these was a third element, the medium of advertising. Just as more or less adolescent players were watching the successor of Indiana Jones jump across their screens, a very different Lara Croft was appearing on billboards and in magazine advertising: a Lara who began to take on a life of her own as that sexy advertising figure recruited by other media; a Lara who, as *Tomb Raider* fans angrily protested, had nothing to do with the game.[3]

(5)

Medial Origins and Sexual Grounds

t is difficult to separate Lara Croft's medial origins from her sexual ones. This is tied to the fact that fascination for the virtual woman is based on a medial bonding that simultaneously inflames desire while making possible her production in the first place. Lara Croft's sexual origins are, in other words, also the grounds of her medial origins. By way of tracking down Lara Croft's medial origins—and the sexual grounds interwoven within them—I would like to start with the particular methodological assumptions of media studies, ones whose contours Marshall McLuhan nicely delineates in his 1964 study *Understanding Media:*

> The concentric with its endless intersection of planes
> is necessary for insight. In fact, it is the technique of
> insight, and as such is necessary for media study, since
> no medium has its meaning or existence alone, but only
> in constant interplay with other media.[1]

McLuhan's media theory contains three central claims, all of which bear a direct relation to the Lara Croft phenomenon:

media are prostheses or extensions of human sensory organs; the medium itself represents its own message; every medium contains another. For McLuhan, a medium is characterized by two functions. On the one hand it stores and accelerates information. On the other it translates a (medially shaped) experience into new form. In this second function, the medium acts as an active metaphor, while the whole medial system forms a single chain of metaphors.[2] Accordingly, McLuhan's famous statement that the medium is the message can be formulated in two ways. Put negatively, it means that the medium lacks a message; put positively, it means that the message of the medium does not represent something outside the medial itself but reveals "the change of scale or pace or pattern that it introduces into human affairs."[3] In this sense, the medium's content is itself a medium, albeit a different one. McLuhan explains:

> This fact [to be without a message], characteristic of all media, means that the "content" of any medium is always another medium. The content of writing is speech, just as the written word is the content of print, and print is the content of the telegraph.[4]

In light of McLuhan's observations, one must ask: If Lara Croft is a medium, then what is her message? What medium is her content? To answer these questions, one must return to the conditions out of which she originated. I have already mentioned how the development of 3-D graphics cards made the PC an ideal vehicle for video games. And it was the capability of these cards that allowed software developers to design games whose appearance resembled that of film. To find the key to understanding the message of Lara Croft, one must, I submit, start looking here—at the connection between Lara Croft and film.

As we already know, Lara Croft was modeled after a Hollywood figure. Listening to the way Jeremy Heath-Smith tells it, the transformation of Indiana Jones into Lara Croft was simply due to concerns that similarities between a male protagonist and his Hollywood prototype "could cause trouble with George Lucas."[5] And how better to camouflage the similarity than by simply changing the game figure's sex? Toby Gard, the lead graphic artist on the *Tomb Raider* development team, was supposed to have responded to Heath-Smith's concerns by drawing up a female version of Indiana Jones. Describing his reaction to Gard's creation, Heath-Smith said:

> I looked with amazement at the screen and said
> something like: "My God, that's a woman. You can't be
> fucking serious." But Toby Gard was enthusiastic, and
> you have to give creative individuals their freedom—
> the freedom to follow what they believe in.[6]

What Gard believed in was a vision of employing new technology to create a game that could be played as a "real-time interactive movie."[7] As one of the many home pages devoted to Lara Croft has commented, of all the different characters that Gard drew up, the one most suitable for fulfilling his vision was a woman.[8] While all male figures inevitably ended up looking like Arnold Schwarzenegger, only a woman, the author of the home page writes, could stand out from the crowd. Yet a figure resembling Schwarzenegger could have made for a good interactive hero as well. So one must ask: What does it mean to stand out from the crowd, and why was doing so important?

Both accounts, the one from Heath-Smith and the one from the home page's author, agree that a male character would have been associated with a *particular* name (Indiana Jones or Arnold Schwarzenegger) and, consequently, with an *identifiable* story. In both it was this association that made a male character unsuitable for *Tomb Raider*. Yet there appears to be a contradiction between the view that male figures would have been identified with a specific personality and the claim that only a female could stand out from the crowd. After all, the individual is generally considered the inverse of the crowd, while the concept of the crowd itself all too often connotes the feminine. This brings us to the question of Lara Croft's femininity. Why is a female figure better suited than a male one to announce the message of the new medium? The answer lies in the particular universality required by a universal medium: a universality that represents both everything and nothing.

An explanation as to why only a female figure can take on the function of a "cultural icon" in the new media society can be found in Teresa de Lauretis's reading of a short passage from Italo Calvino's *Invisible Cities*. In the first chapter of *Alice Doesn't: Feminism, Semiotics, Cinema,* de Lauretis quotes a passage from the founding tale of the city of Zobeide, which Calvino recounts in his novel's third chapter, "Cities and Desire." According to the tale, Zobeide owes its founding to a wonderful dream, one that bears a striking resemblance to the experience of playing *Tomb Raider:*

> Men of various nations had an identical dream. They saw a woman running at night through an unknown city, she was seen from behind, with long hair, and she was naked. They dreamed of pursuing. As they twisted and turned, each of them lost her. After the dream they set out in search of that city; they never found it, but

they found one another; they decided to build a city like the one in the dream.[9]

De Lauretis explains that the city represents the dream woman while, at the same time, the dream woman is the ground for that representation. She stands out from the multiplicity of countable individuals, from the crowd, because instead of being individual she remains alone, incommensurable and not of this world.

In a circular movement resembling the endless intersection of concentric forms that McLuhan uses to characterize media, the woman is the dreamed-for object of desire and the grounds on which—and because of which—the city is built. De Lauretis writes:

> She is both the source of the drive to represent and its ultimate, unattainable goal. Thus the city, which is built to capture men's dream, finally only inscribes woman's absence. The founding tale of Zobeide . . . tells the story of the production of woman as text.[10]

At another point, de Lauretis characterizes this dream woman using imagery still more evocative of Lara Croft's origins:

> By "woman" I mean a fictional construct, a distillate from diverse but congruent discourses dominant in Western cultures (critical and scientific, literary or juridical discourses), which works as both their vanishing point and their specific condition of existence.[11]

De Lauretis compares the importance of the dream woman for constituting societal reality with the function of "the future" in science fiction. Both are speculations toward whose infinitely

receding points the present, from a particular perspective, con-
structs itself.[12]

This brings us back to our original question, for de
Lauretis's observation makes plain the crucial difference between
the anonymity of a figure characterized by her femininity and the
anonymity of those who disappear into the crowd. It is a difference revealed in the dizzying dual sense of woman being both
the source of desire to represent *something* and the medium
through which that desire is objectified. Unlike individuals who
disappear into the multitude, the imagined figure of woman
stands over the crowd because—and only so long as—she remains beyond its reality. The dream woman is above compari-
son, a speculation, one that, as exemplified in the founding tale
of Zobeide, is otherworldly and, for that very reason, grounds
the future as "reality." "Real" women, in contrast, are constituted
by the multiplicity of individual, different women. In finding
a linguistic equivalent to capture the difference between these
women—the many, individual, various, real, and mortal ones—
from the imagined dream woman, de Lauretis distinguishes
between *woman* in the singular and *women* in the plural. This
distinction is important, for, as de Lauretis makes clear, any
feminist reading of cultural texts that understands itself as
operating from a critical perspective must transform representation into performance. To move beyond the imaginary figure
of woman and break her spell, texts must be parried by reen-
acting the assumptions that lie beneath their surface. The spell
of this imaginary dream woman is grounded in the same logic
that makes her into an object of desire: the promise of a fulfilled
ideal reality. Out of this logic emerges a rivalry between the
dream woman and individual women for the "true" reality, a
rivalry that threatens to devalue the reality of the multiplicity of

women. According to de Lauretis, this process must be halted and broken up by exposing the dream woman's origins. The history of those origins demonstrates that the dream woman is a representation that by no means serves the interests of women. It shows that *woman* is neither the ideal of *women* nor an image with which they coincide. De Lauretis concludes, "To perform the terms of the production of woman as a text, as image, is to resist identification with that image."[13]

The closer one looks, the more complicated the relationship becomes between woman and women. Instead of being individual, *woman* stands alone, immortal, incommensurable, ideal, and universal. She is an object of desire precisely because she remains beyond reality, precisely because she—paradoxically—promises a reality beyond reality. The ensuing rivalry between "ideal" reality and "real" reality thus becomes a contest between woman and individual women. The strategic and intellectual demands of this contest are high. As de Lauretis emphasizes above all else, woman draws her own reality only by erasing the difference between herself and women, by making all women into *woman*. Homogenized in this way, women become the point of reference for the dream woman produced as text. The female bodies through which woman is incarnated and by which her immortality is ensured must be plural, and they must be identical, for without them woman no longer stands alone. Instead of being more than all individuals, instead of being every woman and no woman, instead of being everything and nothing, *woman* without *women* simply becomes *no one* and *nothing*.

As I will later show, this discomforting rivalry for "true reality" repeats itself in the relationship between Lara Croft and her real-life models. In the case of Lara Croft, however, that rivalry is enacted on another stage or—in keeping with game parlance—on another level. Among the reasons for this difference is that in Lara Croft, woman produced as text assumes a three-dimensionality, perhaps even a four-dimensionality. Lara Croft as woman has become—to borrow a term from Donna Haraway—a cyborg, one that emerges at the juncture between automaton and autonomy.[14]

Lara Croft offered developers at Core Design a surface on which and with which to realize Gard's vision of a game as a "real-time interactive movie." In doing so, Core Design not only used available technologies but developed new ones as well. The Lara Croft team designed its own 3-D engine and programmed a map editor with which organic-like spaces and structures could be generated. For many of the images, real photos were scanned and used as so-called textures, which were then placed over digitally produced polygonal objects. Lara herself began as a series of pencil sketches and color illustrations. Her dimensions were then entered into a computer, where they were meshed together into a female form made up of thousands of tiny triangles. From there, she was animated using a 3-D wire model and a computer to calculate her intermediate movements. Simulated in real time, Lara's interactions with her environment were designed to give the game a lifelike feel.[15]

Tomb Raider leads off with a video sequence accompanied by music. The player gets carried away as he or she watches an unconscious Lara slide through a tunnel into a dark tomb. As Randi Gunzenhäuser has observed, from the outset of *Tomb Raider* one is forced to assume a "passive, receptive role, as in film."[16] After the video sequence, the game begins, and the player navigates Lara through the various levels via a keyboard or joystick, watching her movements from the perspective of an imaginary camera. Among the game's graphic innovations was the integration of dynamic perspective; that is, the position of rooms and structures adjusts to the movement of the imaginary camera. Although "cutscenes" between levels show frontal views of Lara, during the game she is seen only from behind. For her fans, watching Lara Croft from behind is just as much a myth as her short, high-pitched sigh when she surfaces from the water or picks up one of the health packs lying on the ground. Moving gracefully through all dangers, Lara seems almost delicate. It has often been commented that she arouses the protective instincts of male players, adolescent and adult alike.

The player's gaze follows Lara, follows her movements, which he or she manipulates. With increasing skill, both movements—those of the player and those of Lara—begin to merge. The more virtuoso the player, the more he or she sees through the eyes of Lara. The game draws its power from the exchange of gazes between player and figure, gazes that do not cross but melt into one.[17]

The various features of *Tomb Raider*—the player's passive role, the game's dynamic perspective, the merging of Lara's gaze with that of the player—lend one to conclude that its message, its content, is the interactive movie. Lara plays the part of the medium that inspired and made possible the realization of this message, just like the woman in the dream of Calvino's story. That the Lara Croft medium is likewise "female" is, as we have seen, no accident but follows the logic of the universal medium itself.

6

Virtual Reality

In *Understanding Media,* McLuhan points out the distinctiveness of the movie as a medium. Film, he writes, represents the "spectacular wedding of the old mechanical technology and the new electric world."[1] In England the movie theater was originally called the bioscope because of its "visual presentation of the actual movements of the forms of life," so that "the mechanical appear[ed] as organic."[2] "By sheer speeding up the mechanical," McLuhan tell us, "[the movie] carried us from the world of sequence and connections into the world of creative configuration and structure."[3] He thus concludes, "The message of the movie medium is that of transition from lineal connections to configurations."[4] This nimbly written sentence has far-reaching consequences, for it means nothing other than that the projection of images in quick succession creates the effect of organic-seeming configurations.[5] With the emergence of movies, "we return to the inclusive form of the icon."[6]

If film can make the mechanical itself seem organic—living—by simply speeding up the mechanical, then the question arises as to how this effect is potentiated through the "real-time interactive movie" of video games like *Tomb Raider*. In following the history of Lara Croft, one cannot help but suspect that the message of the interactive movie is the transition from a world of creative configuration and structure to one of autonomously acting gestalts and virtual reality.

"Virtual" is a term used in optics to designate images whose light rays do not actually emanate from where their source seems to be. The philosopher Sybille Krämer has used one type of virtual image—the mirror image—to give a lucid explanation of what we must understand by the word "virtual." Mirror images are virtual, Krämer writes, because they lead their viewer into believing that "the reflected objects are located behind the mirror surface."[7] The apparent positioning of objects behind the mirror brings about a crucial increase in perspectives. We can view reflected objects from the side or even from behind and thus see things otherwise impossible without mirrors. As a further illustration of the expression "virtual world" or "virtual reality," Krämer proposes a thought experiment in which we imagine a mirror "that we can enter and with whose mirror world we can interact."[8] Such an interaction with mirror images requires, as Krämer further explains, that images have the status of sign-event. In other words, we can begin to interact with mirror images only when they function as signs. To be signs, mirror images must in turn be independent of their referent and capable of alteration. Although typical mirror images do not possess these properties,[9] the images of virtual reality do, for they are already in the service of symbolic representations. Krämer defines virtual reality as "a technology for making interactive reflections of symbolic worlds possible."[10] The new perspective that springs out of this kind of symbolic reflection takes place in "an interactive—possibly even synesthetic—contact with data structures."[11] This sounds more complicated than it is, especially since we have already integrated such interactive and synesthetic contact into our everyday lives. This includes, for instance, viewing and changing three-dimensional images on the computer screen as well as listening to music from loudspeakers connected to the PC and manipulable via keyboard, mouse, or microphone. Behind these letters, images, and sounds are data structures that have been translated into perceptible sensation with the help of output units such as printer, screen, and loudspeakers. "With virtual realities," Krämer concludes, "possible worlds can be explored through the senses."[12]

Here we arrive at the point where the hidden difficulties of so-called virtual reality (as well as those of virtual sexuality) have their origin. "Virtual" is not only used in optics but also has a second sense in modal logic—the analysis of the relationship between the categories "necessary," "possible," and "contingent." In this context, "virtual" refers to the realm of the possible, but not of the necessary, and thus stands for the contingent or accidental. As Elena Esposito argues, the virtual makes up the realm of "nonactualized possibilities."[13] If we apply this definition to the one proposed by Krämer, the distressing part of virtual reality becomes clear. For if virtual realities refer to the exploration of possible worlds through the senses, it must then be asked whether that "exploration through the senses" doesn't consist in the very actualization whose absence Esposito describes as the defining feature of virtuality. At the point where data structures can be explored *through the senses,* they can also be *experienced.* They can be seen, heard, and, with the appropriate technical equipment, felt. One can move in them, and—in the double sense of the word plainly exemplified by Lara

Croft—one is moved by them. But that which can be experienced in this way is also perceived as real. With the possibility of real interaction with virtual worlds, not only does the status of virtuality become questionable, but that of reality as well.

For Steven Poole, author of the video game history *Trigger Happy,* the difference between conventional pictures painted in three-dimensional perspective and video game figures composed of multiple polygons is that video game polygons move. Video games thus create not only a physical space but a temporal one as well. This is why Poole concludes that every 3-D game must be understood as four-dimensional. Now, with the introduction of the fourth dimension, the mirror comes into play again. This time, though, as Poole shows using a sequence from *Tomb Raider,* the mirror confronts us with virtual reality's paradox from the other side. In the scene to which Poole refers, the player suddenly encounters a figure who seems to materialize from nowhere, perfectly imitating Lara's every move. The player instinctively thinks the figure is an enemy and shoots until Lara is suddenly shown standing before a large mirror. It then becomes obvious that the supposed enemy is her/his/our/Lara's reflection, a mirror image in the mirror world.[14]

What we have established thus far is that the transformation of data structures into a mirror world perceptible through the senses results in the tendency of virtual realities to cast off their virtuality and take on reality. This tendency explains the obstinacy with which the paradoxical term "virtual reality" asserted itself against the will of those who helped create it. Because some researchers at MIT and the University of North Carolina thought the term too unscientific, too metaphorical, or even absurd, they suggested replacing it with "virtual environment" or "virtual world." What these researchers didn't consider or perhaps didn't want to admit is that by renaming the term they do not escape its paradox. "Virtual environments" and "virtual worlds" only "exist"—even as mere objects of scientific observation—when they are recognized as such and consequently granted the status of sign-events. For the user, signs are symbolic representations. The production of virtual worlds is thus embedded in the process of perception and symbolization from the start. As we know from Jacques Lacan, symbolization processes are predicated on structures of desire and as such are inseparably allied with fantasies and arational wishes. Thus it is not the term "virtual reality" that leads to confusing speculations; these speculations are produced by the technologies of virtual reality themselves. What is disconcerting is the effect that results from tying data structures to structures of desire. It is an effect illustrated by the Chinese puzzle in which Lara Croft appears simultaneously as wholly insipid pixel porridge and fantasy-arousing dream woman.

If reflections or projections can function as signs with which we interact, then in a certain sense they themselves become autonomous. They make contact with us just as much as we do with them. "Interaction with virtual worlds" means nothing other than that. Virtual realities are real in ambiguous ways, but they produce distinctly real effects. In particular, these effects demonstrate that the consequences of the so-called visualization—the creation of visual worlds via digital media— have by no means been adequately grasped. This advance in innovative technology, in whose wake the video game market developed, has been rightly described as the "second computer revolution."[15] The phenomenon of Lara can be considered a result—a child, so to speak—of this revolution.

7

The Interactive Movie

"**V**irtual reality" is a general term for diverse technologies allowing data structures to be experienced through the senses. Experiencing *Tomb Raider*'s particular kind of virtual reality does not require players to put on a data suit or a head-mounted display or enter a so-called CAVE.[1] To see and hear Lara Croft, players need only immerse themselves in the game's interactive movie experience and work the controls of the computer or console.

Along with differentiating the various technologies for producing virtual realities, one must also take into account differences among the game worlds themselves. Different games make possible different forms of interaction. Equipped with multiplayer modes and network capabilities, games such as *Diablo* or the legendary *Half-Life: Counter-Strike* can be played on the Internet by thousands of players throughout the world. *Tomb Raider,* by contrast, is designed for only one player, its interaction limited to that between the user and Lara Croft. It does not foster the development of social skills in the way that role-playing games—whose actors include not only bots but other human beings—potentially can.

In his article "Being Lara Croft," Mike Ward sets forth the rules governing interaction with Lara, explaining, from a male perspective, how much those rules are intertwined with identificatory and narcissistic elements. Ward begins by asking how being Lara Croft differs from being the hero of *Doom*, one of the original first-person shooters developed in the early 1990s. In *Doom* the player is a marine deployed on Mars whose job it is to kill as many aliens as possible in the shortest amount of time. Slipping into the body of the marine, as it were, the player experiences his or her surroundings and opponents from the position of the protagonist. Ward argues that the crucial difference between the heroes of *Doom* and *Tomb Raider*—aside from the greater nuance afforded to Lara Croft—lies in the player's viewpoint. While players of *Doom* see only the marine's arm (which holds a phallic, superlethal weapon), players of *Tomb Raider* see a whole figure, a Lara who is "self-possessed in her hip-swaying walk but spry and potent when she leaps and scrambles . . . [with] the build of a rock-climber and the carriage of an elegant socialite."[2]

The player's interaction with Lara Croft occurs on several levels. The first level of interaction begins with a training session conducted by Lara herself, in which the player is taught how to move and what keys or buttons to press. Following Lara's instructions requires time and patience, along with undivided attention. But this is necessary if the player wants to enjoy the game, if he or she wants to have an automatic, reflex-like mastery of the controls. Only then can the player turn his or her attention to the second level of interaction with Lara Croft, one that, Ward argues, initiates the player into the pleasures of a unique, narcissistic contract:

Lara can climb hand-over-hand, crawl, backflip, tuck
and roll, and lower herself down steep drops. The player
must learn how to "do" these things, and if Lara never
returns the ever-present look, she demonstrates her
awareness of the player in other ways: her only spoken
word is a terse, slightly impatient "no" if you try to
make her perform a move that isn't possible. To the
novice player at an impasse, there seems to be a
frustrated potentiality in the way she stands and
breathes, the user's ineptitude holding all her agility and
lethality at bay. In her poised impatience, she teaches.
Eventually, when the cntl, alt, ins, and end keys become
second nature, this impatience vanishes. There are no
more impasses, only a fluid, reflex connection, a
virtuosity that seems to put Lara and the player both in
the same body, so that it's no longer clear which is the
origin of her performances.

   And even if she incorporates my banality,
my ordinariness, still, she's beautiful. The player's gaze
is a strange closed circle of the desiring look and the
beautiful, powerful exhibition. In fact, the look and
the exhibition are one and the same, bound into a
single, narcissistic contract safer and more symmetrical
than anything Leopold von Sacher-Masoch was ever
able to dream up.

   Damn. No wonder *Tomb Raider*'s so popular.[3]

Fusion with the dream woman presupposes fusion with the
machine. As its beckoning reward, the dream woman arouses
the requisite mechanical mastery of the game.

Another crucial aspect to interaction with Lara Croft is *Tomb Raider*'s filmic quality, or "third-person 3-D style." As Steven Poole has observed, this style, unlike that of the first-person shooter in *Doom,* comes not from painting but from the cinema, where the perspective is that of the camera:

> The player's point of view is explicitly defined, as we saw, as that of a "camera," whose movements can often be controlled as if the player were a phantom movie director, floating about on an invisible crane.[4]

In contrast to strategic and role-playing games developed especially for the PC, *Tomb Raider* borrows, in terms of both graphic layout and story line, closely from Hollywood. Core Design's stated goal of producing an interactive movie is reflected not only in the game's medial kinship to Indiana Jones but also in its passive mode of reception. This proximity to the Hollywood film culminates in Lara Croft herself, who, as *Tomb Raider*'s heroine, resembles a female movie star resurrected in a new medium. Lara Croft is the means through which the film medium and its mode of reception are incorporated into *Tomb Raider*—an incorporation that plays a larger role in *Tomb Raider* than in other action-adventure games. By employing new media technologies capable of producing digital environments, *Tomb Raider* reactivates the whole range of perceptions acquired in the movie theater.

This mode of reception also recurs to the gaze of (Hollywood) cinema, one that not only is based on a conservative view of what distinguishes the masculine and feminine but also—as feminist film criticism of the last twenty-five years has shown—establishes a traditional metaphysics of gender on a new level of abstraction. In this order of perception, "seeing" is imagined as masculine, the viewer as the male. "Being seen" characterizes the position represented by the image of woman, the "eye-catcher" that Teresa de Lauretis calls a dream woman, a speculation set against the multiplicity of women. It is the same metaphysics of gender that I presented in chapter 2, according to which the masculine evokes autonomy, activity, form, and identity, while the feminine, as the inverse of the masculine, stands for heteronomy, passivity, and—as Aristotle wrote of matter—mediality itself.[5]

In her incisive 1975 essay "Visual Pleasure and Narrative Cinema," Laura Mulvey argues that narrative film grounds the position of the (active) male gaze on the concept of woman as (passive) raw material.[6] She begins with the claim that cinema satisfies scopophilic desire—the original wish for pleasurable looking—while simultaneously developing its narcissistic aspect. Cinema, in other words, uncovers two contradictory structures of pleasurable looking: a voyeurism that arises from stimulation through sight, and a narcissism that grows out of the identification with the image seen. In explaining the connection between voyeurism and narcissism, Mulvey draws on Jacques Lacan's understanding of the mirror stage in the formation of the I.[7] Lacan argues that in the mirror stage the child perceives itself as an image, that is to say, as a complete, perfect, "round" gestalt. Inherent in this process of recognizing oneself in the mirror, however, is a misrecognition of self, for the child is *not* the perfection he or she sees in the reflection. Beyond the mirror the child is needy as before, dependent on the mother, unable to realize the autonomy and distinction reflected in the mirror. At the same time, the perfection in which the child imagines himself or herself during the pleasurable observation of the mirror image is necessary for development. For Lacan, the moment of misrecognition is an indispensable part of the I's formation.

According to Mulvey, the key to cinema's having become a site of narcissistic and voyeuristic pleasure is the fact that the image constitutes the matrix of the imaginary. It is only this transfer of the matrix of the imaginary onto cinema that can explain why the image of woman satisfies the contradictory structures of pleasurable looking. Insofar as it is seen, the image of woman provides voyeuristic pleasure as the object and stimulus of sexual desire. Insofar as it reflects the perfection of the mirror, the image of the woman awakens narcissistic desire as the supernatural beauty of the female star, such as that represented by Marlene Dietrich. This dual function, Mulvey explains, cannot be fulfilled by cinema unless the image is a woman, for only the feminine can represent the traumatic threat of castration that precedes fetishism and triggers a twofold investment [*Besetzung*] of libidinal energy in the image. In the gaze defined by narrative film, woman represents voyeuristic desire and the ego ideal of the mirror stage. Her beauty represents the image in the same sense as the matrix of the imaginary. In that perfect beauty, she stands for that which she lacks, the female phallus. She becomes a body fetish, one who, as Freud so aptly remarked, remains well preserved, "doubly derived from contrary ideas."[8]

This dual inheritance has been passed on to the phenomenon of Lara Croft. To realize the extent of that ambiguity, we need only recall the brown braid swinging suggestively to her movements, a braid that played no small role in the game's success and Lara's fame. Although *Tomb Raider* took advantage of film's familiar mode of reception to bring the new medium to a larger public, the recognition of that mode of reception would not have taken place without its heroine. Lara Croft became a star because *Tomb Raider,* unlike the more complicated and less familiar worlds of games such as *Baldur's Gate,* functions as an interactive—hence potentiated—movie. Helping Lara's rise all the more was the fact that her oversize feminine attributes already supplied her with the prerequisites to stardom. One can easily see how cleverly the Lara Croft medium brings its message of the interactive movie to its male audience. As I will show hereafter, the medium is no less successful in delivering that message to its female audience.

For Ward, the appeal of being Lara Croft is grounded in an ever more refined combination of oppositions that, tied to a fetish, integrate the player into a closed cycle of narcissism and voyeurism. The interactive movie format potentiates the bind between the one who is looking at/playing with the seen object to the point where the difference between the two objects collapses. One sees and is seen; one sees himself or herself in the object. Moreover, one sees in the object his or her actual or better or true self. Voyeurism and exhibitionism coincide; one is at once man and woman. The individual satisfies his or her own self.

By way of illustration, let me cite a short Internet dialogue between two *Tomb Raider* players:

> FIRST PERSON: And about Lara Croft: yeah, she's got big tits, but the game's still thought out, it's not just about monster tits.
>
> SECOND PERSON: I think so too. She also has a wonderful and well-animated ponytail [*Pferdeschwanz*].[9]

In sum, the interaction with Lara Croft acclimatizes the public to the medium of the computer by making use of the familiar cinematic mode of reception. Unlike movie audiences, however, players of *Tomb Raider* must first acquire this mode of reception by previously having mastered the controls of the new medium. The pleasure of playing a game relying on this mode of reception is only truly achieved when the player's skill allows the keyboard or controller to fade from consciousness. Without this awareness, the knowledge that playing Lara Croft involves the synesthetic implementation of data structures also disappears. The merging of player and machine is not only the condition on which one can enter into the pleasure of Ward's narcissistic contract. That merging also triggers and sustains an active forgetting, first with respect to Lara Croft's medial or mechanical nature, second with respect to the narcissistic enjoyment that her presence provides.

If, as McLuhan has written, figures come alive on the movie screen, then virtual figures not only come alive but assert autonomy, that is, take on a life of their own. Like Haraway's cyborgs existing at the juncture between automaton and autonomy, virtual figures emerge from the hardware to lay claim on reality beyond the screen. It is a process that adheres to the logic concealed in the technology of virtual realities, a logic that, in Sybille Krämer's words, consists in "making interactive reflections of symbolic worlds possible."

One of the functions of this technology is to create a rift in the screen-viewing subject. In the world behind the screen, he or she encounters figures that owe their creation to a sign-event even as they are more/different than signs. They are figures who, originating at the point where automaton meets autonomy, act automatically. As such, they become our intimate friends—at least that's what an Internet "Star Portrait" of Lara Croft suggests: "Lara Croft is a magical woman. For many she is closer than good friends and realer than most relatives."[10] As projection screens for the various wishes and fantasies of their fans, virtual figures not only are "more human" than many of their fellow human beings but also hold a decisive advantage over them: virtual figures, even in the bloodiest of battles, are not *really* vulnerable. Withstanding every injury, supplied with many lives, capable of infinite resurrections, they live without being mortal. In one of her first interviews, the virtual Lara Croft was asked what she thought about being an imaginary figure. Her response:

> Well, it gives me a touch of immortality. I also think
> that the graphics people from Core Design have given
> me quite an attractive look—don't you think so?
> Although it still feels unusual to me to see my face
> on the title pages of computer magazines, I'm getting
> used to it.[11]

This touch of immortality in a beautiful female body also accommodates women's fantasies of power. One does not, in other words, need to be a man to take up the "male" position of the viewer.[12] But this shouldn't imply that sex plays no role. Not every action-adventure game gives boys and girls, women and men, a figure with whom they can identify. Lara Croft's special talent lies in her ability to reflect the "true" and "better self" of both sexes, therefore strengthening the identity of each.

For girls, Angela McRobbie argues, it is especially important that Lara "fits into the pre-pubertal dream of being unconstrained by gender."[13] Lara must never "reflect on her position or identity or image in relation to the 'male gaze.'" Like the players who identify with her, Lara Croft is liberated from the controlling gaze of men. Female players interact with Lara Croft in the same privacy and intimacy as do *Tomb Raider*'s male players. Randi Gunzenhäuser gives a more detailed description of how females perceive this interaction:

> Lara lets me practice, with her, again and again until
> I am ready to advance with her to the next level. . . .
> [Players] get positive kicks and positive feedback: I can
> make it to the next level, I can make it. . . . That's
> important, especially in adolescence, but later on, too,
> when one is up against one's own feeling of insecurity.[14]

Gunzenhäuser emphasizes Lara's autonomy, her action, her adventurousness, and above all her independence. Lara Croft is supposed to possess all these qualities while also being a woman, a fact Gunzenhäuser thinks makes Lara better than any male hero. Yet in the schema of heterosexual dualism, these qualities go under the heading "male." By appropriating them, Lara Croft makes men—at least in the form produced by the order of the sexes—superfluous. Just as with male players, the interaction with Lara Croft proves to be a hermetic cycle. The female player, like her male counterpart, becomes at once man and woman:

> As for girls and women—and I am no exception—Lara
> conveys an added sense of security. Many women I have
> talked to stress the importance of Lara's complete inde-
> pendence, the fact that, as a woman, she copes with
> adversity masterfully, performing heroic acts in the
> world of adventure, while at home she is a total failure.
> Hearth and home aren't where she belongs. She belongs
> to the big wide world: in the jungle, in caves, and in the
> mountains, that is to say, dangerous places, places that
> are still out of bounds for women, even today. Lara
> fights her way through a man's world. Her adventures

are the adventures of a James Bond or an Indiana Jones,
men's adventures through and through. She is better
than all those males heroes, though. Don't we all want
to be like that sometimes?[15]

The refusal of the housewife role may allow the reorientation of
the feminine ideal, but when that ideal consists in traditional
male values such as independence, courage, and heroism, nothing is changed in the dualistic order of the sexes. However much
Lara Croft acts the role of the better male, she is still a woman.
The hierarchy of values remains as unaffected as its underpin-
nings in the relation between the sexes. The fact that Lara Croft
is a woman with "male" characteristics is seen in her adventurousness, autonomy, and actions. The fact that Lara Croft is a
woman is seen simply by looking at her. Lara Croft's femininity
is reduced, in a very traditional manner, to her oversize female
attributes. One sees her femininity by looking at her, even when
her behavior is masculine through and through. The phenomenon of Lara Croft thus reproduces the law binding femininity to
the body. In view of the fact that Lara Croft is a virtual—utterly
noncorporeal—figure, her instantiation of this law truly borders
on a miracle.

Gunzenhäuser's answer to the question of what kind of
feminism Lara Croft could represent ultimately shows how
much the narcissistic contract binding the female player to the
virtual figure mirrors the one Mike Ward describes as the
(over)fulfillment of male sadomasochistic dreams. For Gunzenhäuser, Lara Croft conveys the message that women must give
everything they have to survive:

What is interesting in the context is, in my opinion, the
way Lara relates to her environment. I love it when she

bangs into walls. The groan she gives is like a war cry. It's as though she's gathering strength for the fight. Lara does not give up. She has immense energy combined with a resilience that makes her bounce right back. You can make her charge against the wall time and time again, and it would do her no harm. Lara knows no pain, and the word "setback" isn't part of her vocabulary—I find that fascinating.

In this sense Lara embodies an important feminist principle: Never give up![16]

But might this description not rather suggest the futility and hopelessness of a feminism conceived in this way?

8

The Loss of Surface

In *The Plague of Fantasies* (1997) Slavoj Žižek argues that technobiology and virtual reality have brought about the "loss of the surface which separates inside from outside."[1] In light of my work on Lara Croft thus far, this claim merits further consideration, for connected with this "loss of surface" is an erasure of the border between inside and outside, self and other, behind the screen and before the screen, the world on this side of the mirror's surface and the world beyond. It is a process consisting of the same closed, narcissistic contract described by Mike Ward in his analysis of the *Tomb Raider* experience. This contract might also be characterized as a short circuit, one that, by eliminating the distance between self and virtual projection, severs the connections to external world and other subjects alike. As in the tale of Narcissus, the subject vanishes in the indecidability between self and reflected image. The loss of surface is tantamount to a loss of distance, and without distance there is neither knowledge nor "appearances." Players no longer want to distinguish between themselves and Lara.

"Loss of surface" should not imply that a clear dividing line between truth and appearance, reality and fiction, so-called real life and virtual reality can or should be drawn. Psychoanalysis in particular has taught that the reality connecting us with others, the reality we share with others, is a *symbolic* order whose existence presupposes the faculty of imagination. There is, in other words, no reality without the collaboration of fantasy. But as our experience with Lara Croft has also demonstrated, acknowledging reality's dependence on fantasy does not diminish the need to distinguish between the reality we share with others and our own desires. This is what makes the matter of reality so complicated.

Instead of overcoming this loss of surface, Žižek asks that we face it head on. Doing so means recognizing the ambiguity inherent in virtuality's origins. "Virtual," Žižek writes, refers both to

> the virtual status of phantasmic reality we perceive on the interface's surface *and* to the pure calculation that cannot be reduced to its materialization of electric current passing through computer chips.[2]

This is the same ambiguity we have already encountered with Lara Croft. On the one hand, virtual reality involves an exploration of data structures through the senses; on the other, it is an effect constituted by desire and human imagination. Facing this loss of surface means standing and withstanding the ambiguity that emerges from the wedding of data structures with structures of desire. It means refusing to reduce ambiguity to some purported univocal standpoint.

The common tendency, however, is to do just that. One popular view demotes virtual reality to mere fantasy, and another elevates it to the matrix of everything real. In the case of the former, virtual reality gets strictly separated from "real life" and made into its opposite. Consisting of the natural world, "real life" is fashioned into the one and true reality. In the case of the latter, the everyday world appears merely as an alternative window of virtual reality—a window that seldom has the better view. For those who see virtual reality this way, fulfillment takes place not in the natural world but in the simulacral worlds of cyberspace. Yet when all realities are declared virtual, the only criterion of truth remaining is degree of wish fulfillment.[3] More than making everything virtual, this kind of view makes "real life" itself seem less fulfilled, less authentic than those windows that open out to the deep recesses of the cyberspace universe.

In truth both views are equally reductive, each more a trap than an alternative. Both are based, according to Žižek, on a "kind of foreclosure of the Real."[4] In Lacanian psychoanalysis, the Real stands for the facticity of things that cannot be captured by symbolization. The Real confronts us with time and death and becomes noticeable in the *horror vacui* that shows the idea of a world where all wishes find fulfillment to be a phantasm. It acts as a sobering correction to imaginary identification, thwarting its closed cycle and creating a fracture that interrupts the identification with the simulacrum and allows entrance into the symbolic order. The Real shows identification with the imaginary to be nothing more than illusory. Yet it is precisely the power of the Real and its participation in the symbolic order—where each of us is recognized and given recognition as an other—that both of these views ignore. Conflating "real life" with virtual reality is predicated just as much on the wish for a true and intact world as the strict distinction between a virtual world and a *Lebenswelt* conceived as natural and immediate.

Both rest firmly on the phantasm of what could be called a "fulfilled reality."

Even if Žižek's reflections on cyberspace take too little notice of the differences between various kinds of interaction and virtual reality, the following example shows how they can nevertheless contribute significantly to our understanding of Lara Croft. In the commercial announcing the release of *Tomb Raider II* titled "Where the Boys Are," the viewer is shown various public spaces where one would expect to find "the boys": men's restrooms, bowling alleys, basketball courts, pool halls, and strip bars. All are empty and abandoned. Since the commercial characterizes "the boys" through their absence, one can't say much for sure about them, as Mike Ward admits in "Being Lara Croft." Yet, he writes, we can figure that

> one of the things they've invested in Lara is their
> sexuality—among the people they've left patronless by
> going home to play *Tomb Raider* is an exotic dancer
> who idly chews gum on the stage of an empty strip
> club. The boys aren't interested in the sex industry's
> gaze exchange anymore. They'd much rather hone their
> puppeteering skills and close the distance between
> themselves and Lara. Not that anyone *knows* the boys—
> the commercials signify them through undribbled
> basketballs and unattended men's rooms. But we all
> know Lara. The commercial's lifeless shots of the physi-
> cal, social world are juxtaposed with tantalizing visual
> nibbles of *Tomb Raider,* Lara sprinting, blasting her
> pistols, rowing her canoe. Where the boys are is inside
> Lara, being her. Staying home and being Lara has one
> up on going out and being oneself.[5]

Being Lara Croft relieves individuals of the burden of confronting their own limits, as well as those placed on them by others. But this fusion does not mean that a separation between virtual reality and real life is required. The crux of Žižek's argument is that a more fundamental distinction must be made, a distinction between "imaginary illusion" and "symbolic fiction." Imaginary illusion, a concept borrowed from Lacan, refers to the process of identificatory fusion with an image, a process that goes hand in hand with the loss of surface. In the case of symbolic fiction, another Lacanian term, that surface, that is, the distance to the projection, is maintained. As such, the symbolic fiction avoids confusing image and truth without necessarily opposing them. It reserves a proper conceptual place for misrecognition—a process so necessary in the formation of the I in Lacanian psychoanalytic theory—and avoids the temptation to see true reality in the reflection of the image's perfection. Unlike the imaginary illusion, the symbolic fiction does not reduce a symbol to a narcissistic identification with a simulacrum. Our commitment to a reality in which we let ourselves and others live, whether inside or outside cyberspace, hangs, like a silk thread, on the ability to distinguish between imaginary illusions and symbolic fictions.[6]

What distinguishes the one from the other? Both are, as Žižek argues, signifiers and as such represent illusory "phallic prostheses."[7] The difference lies in the stance one takes toward these illusions. In the imaginary illusion, an apparent reality is projected onto the virtual mirror image. We see this in the subject's identification with a decentered image like Lara Croft or in the reduction of virtuality's inherent ambiguity to one of those narcissistic short circuits I referred to earlier, where the everyday is either divested of the virtual and claimed as the only true reality or becomes a mere mode of cyberspace. The symbolic fiction, in contrast, "stands for phallus as pure semblance."[8] The idea of a fulfilled reality remains a fantasy without becoming a phantasm of a true and ideal reality. The symbolic fiction resists the temptation to naturalize the phallus, which also means that it resists the temptation to naturalize virtuality. In doing so, it demands that we recognize the impossibility of achieving a fully realized, true, natural, and immediate reality. It demands that we recognize the ambiguity inherent in the duofold origins of *every* reality as an interplay between the real, imaginary, and symbolic. These duofold origins require that we draw a dividing line between illusion and reality while simultaneously rendering such a distinction impossible to make. We thus find ourselves in the paradoxical situation of having to live in a world for which we are structurally inadequate. Yet that which seems to be an insufficiency or blind spot can, from another vantage point, represent the very opening that prevents imaginary closure.[9] Consciousness of this blind spot creates distance between the image and myself. It makes the image into "appearance" and opposes the imaginary illusion. Borrowing again from Lacan, Žižek describes this blind spot as an "elusive point from which the object returns the gaze," without which "we no longer 'see something,'" without which "'reality' itself is perceived as a visual hallucination."[10]

It is this very blind spot that brings the question of sexual difference into play.[11] It is a question that, as Judith Butler has written, characterizes the "necessary background to the possibility of thinking, of language, of being a body in the world."[12] Sexual difference is "not a bedrock of any sorts" but "a question, a question for our times."[13] It is a question that can amaze, one that can make us ask the kinds of questions that cannot be explained in their totality. The question of sexual difference is not a question among others but "a particularly dense moment of irresolution within language." As a gap confronting knowledge with its own irresolvability, sexual difference counteracts, even in scientific and philosophical inquiry, the narcissistic self-mirroring process. Sexual difference is the moment that resists the identification of the signifier with a decentered image, the moment that refuses imaginary closure.

⑨

The Medialization of the Body

U sing Lara Croft and her models as an example, I want to illustrate the dynamics that can be set in motion by the imaginary illusion. As an identification with a decentered image, one that stands in an ambiguous relation to the object it represents and to the way in which it represents, the imaginary illusion does not stop with the narcissistic contract described by Mike Ward. Instead it gives the virtual figure the status of a dream woman who has become real, the one we encountered in the poem cited at the beginning of this book. How does the computer figure become the incarnation of the ideal woman?

The transformation can be said to follow the same process described by Teresa de Lauretis in which *woman* comes to stand over *women*. Yet, as a virtual figure, Lara Croft goes a decisive step further than the woman of the cinematic image. The identification process reaches beyond the imaginary subjugation of the multiplicity of women under an abstract ideal to the point where Lara Croft emerges from the imaginary space of the image and assumes "real" form in the bodies of women.

In supporting the phantasm of a fulfilled, ideal reality, Lara also maintains a heterosexual metaphysics of gender implicit in that phantasm. Contrary to the hopes that some feminists placed in her, Lara Croft promotes the reduction of women to their (female) bodies.

Soon after Lara Croft started appearing simultaneously on computer screens and in magazine and billboard advertisements, executives at Eidos came up with the idea of finding a real woman to incarnate her. The contest they sponsored to determine an official Lara Croft model attracted scores of young women. Applicants' pictures were posted on the Internet, where fans could vote for the woman who reminded them most of Lara Croft.

The first Lara Croft model to be selected was Natalie Cook, who remained relatively unknown. The same can't be said for her successor, Rhona Mitra, the model fired by Eidos after she started to identify with Lara instead of simply being content to lend the idol her body. It was rumored that the twenty-one-year-old had her father, a cosmetic surgeon, enlarge her breasts so as to better approximate Lara's own. By the time Mitra was quoted in an interview as saying, "I understand people are wary about this perfect character being brought to life. But I know that I'm her and it will be all right," Eidos and Core Design had already selected Vanessa Demouy and Nell McAndrew to be the new official Lara Croft models.[1] Yet they too were quickly replaced by others. Lara's managers at Eidos were careful to prevent models from claiming to be the perfect embodiment of Lara—from acquiring dream woman status. Instead of being equated with any one of them, Lara was to stand over all of them. None of the models, that is to say, was to be more than her body. Fitted to and measured with Lara's own, a model's body was only a means for bringing Lara to life. To prevent the "true" immortal Lara from receiving unwanted competition from her real-life embodiments, ones with whom she might be "confused," models were not permitted to serve as the official Lara Croft for more than a year. This policy was in keeping with the composite nature of the figure the models embodied. Because Lara Croft was put together using features of numerous women—the voice from one woman, the breasts from another, the legs and arms from still others—no one could claim to be the original Lara Croft.

The official models had to sign autographs and give interviews, and once, at a promotional event for *Tomb Raider III*, one had to appear covered head to toe in metallic paint.[2] But the pictures of the models make plain what really mattered: supplying the imaginary Lara Croft with a reference, one that lent the ideal woman a "fulfilled" reality. And it is telling that the models represent not the Lara of advertisements but the Lara of the video game. Aside from having to appear in original Lara Croft attire, Nell McAndrew was often photographed baring her teeth just as Lara does in *Tomb Raider II*. (This feature was celebrated as one of the most important technical innovations over the still-expressionless Lara Croft of *Tomb Raider I*.) If McAndrew had appeared in a bikini or a black minidress, instead of Lara Croft's lime green outfit, she would have passed for herself or some other model, but she would not have been identified instantly as Lara Croft. The production of the imaginary illusion depends on an immediate recognition linking Lara Croft to her model.

Lending the virtual figure a body makes the imaginary illusion perfect. It is a process that ultimately leads to imaginary closure: the virtual woman loses her fictional, illusionary character and becomes the representative of an ideal reality. This consummation of the imaginary illusion ensures that images of Lara seen in advertising appear to be photos of a truly existing virtual figure. Indeed, the relationship between Lara Croft and her models follows a simple formula: the more exactly she is copied by her models, the more she can diverge from her "original" video game appearance while still being recognized as the immortal Lara.

The story of Lara and her models adheres to the same logic that underlies those "interactive reflections of symbolic worlds" described by Sybille Krämer. The story is based on a simplification of the ambiguity inherent in the concept of the virtual. Through lending the virtual figure the semblance of a "fulfilled" reality in the bodies of many women, the multiple origins of Lara Croft are concealed. This not only supports the phantasm of an ideal reality but also continues its attendant devaluation of everyday life, a life that connects us to others and reminds us of our limits. In truth, the incarnation of Lara Croft results in a reversal of the relationship between original and copy. Real bodies become, in a perverse way, mere copies that never add up to their supposed original: the dream woman.

If the virtual Lara embodies real life, it only follows that interaction with Lara Croft outside the game takes place directly with the virtual figure rather than through her models. In a television commercial for *Brigitte,* a German women's magazine, Lara Croft was not played by a model but, after time-consuming technical effort, made to appear on-screen as the virtual Lara in person. For all its high-tech production, however, the commercial's message is a traditional one. While in pursuit of an adversary, Lara happens to notice a wedding dress in a shop window. Stopping to admire it and dream of a white wedding, Lara shows us her emotional side.

In the case of Irish band U2, it also seemed that interest in Lara lay only in the reality of her virtuality. In their 1997 "PopMart" tour, U2 had Lara appear on the giant onstage LED screen—52 × 62 m—that accompanied their act. During the hit from the *Batman Forever* sound track, "Hold Me, Kill Me, Kiss Me, Thrill Me," the screen shows Lara as she poses in front of a blue background, climbs on a motorbike, and rides away, only to appear again shortly afterward, this time aiming a rifle at the singers.

(A short aside: the cyberpunk writer William Gibson is said to have had Lara's U2 appearances in mind when he wrote *Idoru,* his novel about a rock star who falls in love with a virtual colleague. William Gibson, of course, is also closely associated with cyberspace. Gibson coined the term—one we can hardly imagine doing without today—in his novel *Neuromancer,* defining cyberspace as a "consensual hallucination." This is a nice example of the recursive relationships in our media world—an interconnectedness that lets us feel at home.)

After Lara Croft's appearance in the U2 tour, numerous bands inquired about enlisting Lara for their concerts, most without success.[3] Lara's popularity was so great, *Lara Croft Magazin* wrote, that even pop stars had become her fans. This remark touches on the crux of Lara's medial success. Guaranteed a point of reference by the bodies of the Lara Croft models, the Lara of advertising distanced herself so much from *Tomb Raider* that true fans felt betrayed and began to boycott the game.[4] They had reason to feel put off. The Lara who conquered the media had in truth nothing more to do with *Tomb Raider.* Just like the video game protagonist and her models, *Tomb Raider* had merely become a way to secure a point of reference for the Lara of advertising.

(10)

The Universal Medium

ara Croft, of whom even pop stars have declared themselves fans, has become a universal medium, a medium that can contain potentially any other. Through Internet, news, radio, dance, television, novels, advertising, and film, the virtual Lara has been transformed into a universal label. Science fiction, comics, and chat rooms live off her just as much as the multinational corporation Eidos. Yet despite her ubiquity, the media have failed to produce the kind of in-depth reporting on the video game world one might expect. In light of what has been presented so far, this may not surprise anyone. It nevertheless demands explanation. The game world represents an important part of society, one in which our children live and grow up. Yet this world remains closed and unknown to most adults, even parents.

Lara Croft served the media as a means for reciprocal reflection. As an icon, the virtual figure unified different media, giving their respective public spheres the one word everyone understood: Lara. This is how Lara became a universal medium that held together media society and served as its mirror image.

Such a multitalented icon cannot be understood as an image in the traditional sense. In the context of computer language, her image should rather be understood as a symbolic element in a system of hieroglyphics, a writing-become-image possessing the magic of enchanted signs. Lara Croft functions as a signifier of "electronic writing." That is to say, she is an icon that displays hypertext links to other texts. Mike Sandbothe illustrates this function in relation to signs, or to letters that function as signs:

> In the Internet, texts and images become icons, i.e., they are programmable as signifiers that, via a pragmatic mouse click, produce a connection to what they signify that is no longer merely symbolic, but real. . . . A mouse click on a sequence of words programmed as a link in a philosophical hypertext can lead me directly to Nietzsche's work. A mouse click on a picture of Friedrich Nietzsche programmed as a link can bring me directly to a Web site with information about the philosopher's life.[1]

As an icon, Lara Croft functions like the Internet texts and images described by Sandbothe. She stands not for an individual abstract meaning but for a reference system. And only an icon of this kind can function as an icon of the new media culture. She is an image generated from digital data structures possessing the magic to create a "real" (in Sandbothe's sense of the word) connection to that which she signifies.[2] Derived from opposites, she signifies everything and nothing, creating the connection to everything and nothing, and fulfilling the wishes and fantasies projected onto her. Lara's status as icon accounts for her many faces and makes up the heart of her medial message.

It is precisely why an analysis of Lara Croft demands a proper foundation in media theory.[3]

Yet even media theorists are still well advised to stay in transdisciplinary contact with gender studies. As the following case shows, anything less could expose them all too easily to the laughter of virtual creations. The example concerns McLuhan's distinction between hot and cold media.[4] Hot media are those that address only one sense and require little personal activity on the part of the user. Hot media such as radio are active and require little participation. Cool media, on the other hand, supply little information and address many senses. As with the telephone, they are themselves generally passive and require the participation of the user. McLuhan ends his analysis with an analogy taken from what he calls a piece of "folk wisdom": "Men seldom make passes at girls who wear glasses."[5] This saying, McLuhan assures us, illustrates the principle according to which hot media can be differentiated from cold. A woman with glasses represents the perfect example of a hot medium, while a woman with sunglasses is the perfect example of a cool medium:

> Glasses intensify the outward-going vision, and fill
> the image exceedingly, Marion the librarian
> notwithstanding. Dark glasses, on the other hand,
> create in the feminine the inscrutable and inaccessible
> image that invites a great deal of participation and
> completion.[6]

McLuhan didn't reckon on Lara Croft, for she represents just that medium which levels both the sexual and medial differences between cool and hot media. It was a talent for which she also received public recognition: the very clever use of her eyewear, especially the provocative way in which she peers out over them directly into the eyes of those interacting with her—a means for increasing what McLuhan calls "outward-going vision"—won her the title of "Female Sunglasses Wearer of the Year" at the Spectacle and Sunglass Wearer of the Year Awards 2000.[7] So we see: even media theorists can learn from gender studies.

Tomb Raider: The Movie

would like to conclude my analysis of Lara Croft as universal medium by briefly considering the first *Tomb Raider* movie. I want to show that the intimacy experienced in the video game by virtue of its real-time interactive format finds its way into the motion picture as well— a quality that helps account for both the movie's strengths and its reputed weaknesses. My analysis will then proceed to the question of what it means for a virtual star to be embodied by a real-life one.

Although *Lara Croft: Tomb Raider* was by no means the first movie to be based on a video game, no previous adaptation had been produced on such a massive budget. Director Simon West was said to have modeled the movie on *Raiders of the Lost Ark* (1981), whose Indiana Jones had served as Lara Croft's cinematic precursor. Like the George Lucas/Steven Spielberg production, *Tomb Raider* was supposed to become another blockbuster Hollywood success. By the time the film was released in the summer of 2001, video game fans, moviegoers, and critics were all in a state of anxious expectation.

West's dream didn't come true. Critics generally thought that *Tomb Raider* lacked the story line of a Hollywood classic. Several remarked that the movie made them feel as if they were watching someone else play a video game, and movie reviewers—quite justifiably—found the film's plot and dialogue unconvincing. For their part, the video and computer game communities accused the director of ignorance. They claimed that West had no firsthand experience with the game and deviated from Lara Croft's official biography.[1] In the movie, Lara's father is an archaeologist who died when she was young, whereas according to the biography provided by Lara's creators, her father is a "normal" British lord, still very much alive and well. One reviewer remarked quite astutely that Lara's emotional attachment to her dead father serves to connect the segments of the movie, with the clues left by the father supplying the narrative impulse for Lara's ultimate mission. The movie's various backdrops—Croft's country estate, Venice, Cambodia, and Iceland—call to mind the levels of a video game. The difference with video games, of course, is that their levels require no narrative continuity; the players pass through them on their own.

All in all, critics thought that Simon West had made a mediocre movie, one that neither kept to the formulas of good Hollywood films nor remained true to the video game on which it was based. Yet for all that, *Tomb Raider* was far from being a flop. Disparaging remarks about script and dialogue notwithstanding, most reviews ended with approval and goodwill. The driving force behind the upbeat conclusions was unanimous enthusiasm for Angelina Jolie's performance as Lara Croft. Some reviews called Jolie a born Lara; others said she transformed the video game figure into a virtual icon for feminine authority and coolness. Encapsulating these views, Roger Ebert wrote, "Here is a movie so monumentally silly, yet so wondrous to look at, that only a churl could find fault."[2]

When Ebert wrote that *Tomb Raider* was "wondrous to look at," he was no doubt referring to the camera's incessant close-ups of Jolie. Against all claims to the contrary, this complete focus on the heroine bespeaks a high degree of faithfulness to the video game experience. That this faithfulness may nevertheless have contributed to the movie's actual weakness emerges quite clearly from a review written for one of Berlin's biweekly magazines. According to the author of the review, West's camera was so "enamored" of the leading actress that other individuals in the movie became insignificant.[3]

The concentration on the movie's heroine to the practical exclusion of all others conforms exactly to the visual architecture of the *Tomb Raider* video game. Eliminating any mediating perspective, this architecture merges the perspective of the viewer and player with that of the camera and places them in sole interaction with the heroine. When the same Berlin film critic adds that one almost feels guilty for the unabashed pleasure of watching Jolie as she shoots, curses, and fights her way through the movie, he is—probably without knowing it—describing the narcissistic form of perception bequeathed to the *Tomb Raider* movie from the interactive movie. Distinguishing *Tomb Raider* from traditional Hollywood films such as *Raiders of the Lost Ark,* this redoubled narcissistic perception accounts for the camera's fixation on Jolie as well as for the enthusiastic reception of her performance. It also explains why the weakness of the film's plot is by no means accidental. The intimate fixation on the heroine inhibits the creation of an exciting story line. Against the backdrop of such a "setting," the plot must compete with the camera's narcissistic gaze.

In one of the first interviews after the film was completed, Jolie was asked whether playing Lara Croft was a dream come true. She replied, "Sure, yeah. I saw the film for the first time yesterday, and all I could think of was how much I miss being her."[4] Jolie is of course not the first movie actor to bring to life a fictional character from another medium. In the 1930s Shirley Temple helped Heidi, the character from Johanna Spyri's children's book, achieve legendary fame, and propelled her own acting career in the process.[5] To this day, the image of the child star with her curly blonde hair and chubby cheeks continues to embody America's image of Heidi. In Terry Zwigoff's *Ghost World* (2000), Thora Birch played Enid Coleslaw, the eighteen-year-old heroine of Daniel Clowes's graphic novel. Birch's performance brought Coleslaw—as well as the director, Clowes, and Birch herself—into the hearts and minds of many a viewer and established her name in film and on the Internet.[6] Yet unlike Jolie, neither Shirley Temple nor Thora Birch could have said afterward how much they miss *being* their respective roles.

The difference is that Jolie does not merely portray a fictional figure; she plays the part of a *virtual star*—a fact that her interview response exploits quite perfectly. By admitting how much she misses being Lara Croft, Jolie appropriates the language of Lara Croft's fans and conforms to their expectations. Jolie acknowledges the reality of Lara Croft's ideality and, in doing so, voluntarily follows the same rule that Eidos imposed on its Lara Croft models: not to compete, identify, or compare oneself with Lara Croft. Later in the same interview, when asked about the size of her breasts, Jolie reaffirms the distinction between herself and the virtual Lara: "Yeah, I'm a 36C, and in the movie she's a 36D and in the game she's a 36DD, so yes, there was some padding."

How does playing a virtual star relate to being a real one? By gearing the *Tomb Raider* game to the appearance of a conventional movie, its developers established a connection with a popular mode of reception, making the computer medium accessible to a large section of the public. At the same time, *Tomb Raider* developers anchored that familiar mode of reception to the experience of the computer medium itself. As in Hollywood movies, the mode of reception in the game is marked by its passivity; the pleasure it offers is primarily voyeuristic. Because interaction between player and computer is concentrated entirely on the feminine heroine, the computer is obliviated, and the distance between player and medium effaced. The fusion with the medium allows the player to forget his or her own body. Instead of fostering a distancing reflection, this fusion conceals the perception-forming effects of the medium, giving the medium a life of its own by way of empathy with the moving image.

It is precisely these aspects that bring to mind the phenomenon of the star and its place in cinematic history. In his introduction to *Star Texts* (1991), Jeremy G. Butler rightly calls attention to the split between the theoretical study of film and the star-driven popular interest that helped establish the industry and make film the most influential medium of the twentieth century.[7] Indeed, for many years, actor performance, stars, and stardom were not objects of serious film studies, which mainly focused on aspects inherent to the medium itself: montage, editing, and camera work, along with the director as "author/artist." This concentration of interest on the technical means of expression goes back to Russian formalism, a school of thought that greatly influenced theoretical reflection on cinema. According to Lev Kuleshov, the founder of the world's first film school, the

sole task of the director was to express meaning through editing and montage. The actor's body, in contrast, was a machine
to be manipulated by the director.

As a result, film theory did not really shape the art of
on-screen performance. Movie actors instead took their cue
from the methods developed by Constantin Stanislavski at the
Moscow Art Theatre, which he helped found in 1897. Trying
to distance contemporary theater from the theatricality of the
nineteenth-century stage, Stanislavski championed a highly nat-
uralistic acting style. Actors were not merely to play their roles;
they were supposed to become them. Unlike Kuleshov, the Russian director Vsevolod I. Pudovkin recognized that Stanislavski's
efforts to bring acting and life closer together were in keeping
with the expectations of movie audiences, who came to see *living* images, stars in action. Pudovkin thus defined the fundamental task of the movie actor as creating a unified and real-life
image. The actor was to embody the living image, breathing life
into cinema itself.

Stanislavski's methods ultimately found their place in
Hollywood film via the Actors Studio, the New York workshop
founded in 1947 and later directed by Lee Strasberg. The big
stars of the 1950s—Marlon Brando, Julie Harris, Montgomery
Clift, James Dean, and Marilyn Monroe, to name but a few—
all studied under Strasberg's tutelage. Just like Stanislavski and
Pudovkin, Strasberg understood the actor's true objective in
using his or her body to invest the cinematic image with reality.

Putting Strasberg's theories into more specific terms,
one could say that for an actor to produce reality, he or she must
transform the discontinuity of editing and montage into continuity. That is to say, the actual task of the actor is to conceal
the meaning-constituting function of the technical apparatus.

The better the actor succeeds in portraying life, the less visible the film as medium becomes; the more invisible the medium, the more visible the star; the greater the star, the easier it is for movie audiences to empathize with the life that the actor portrays.

The concealment of the technical means of expression runs contrary to the cause of experimental cinema, which to this day continues to see the representation of the inherently cinematic as one of its central tasks. Hollywood film not only obscures the technical origin of images but also predetermines a mode of reception in which the viewer is invited to empathize with the life depicted by the star. It is the same passive position created by the *Tomb Raider* game. Instead of active engagement with the medium, the concealment promotes the viewer's fusion with it. From this perspective, the discrepancy between theoretical interest in the technical means of expression and popular interest in the movie star is more than a mere lapse on the part of film studies. Rather, it reflects two antagonistic spheres of interest, one dedicated to those aspects that remain inherent to the medium, the other oriented toward the star-driven Hollywood film industry.

Turning back to the *Tomb Raider* movie, we can see that by putting Jolie in the role of Lara Croft, the makers of the film were following the laws and interests of Hollywood. Those laws and interests demand the highest possible continuity in order to conceal discontinuity, to conceal the technical origin of those images with which one interacts. That Jolie was playing a virtual star only augmented this concealment, for the secret of *Tomb Raider* lies in the fact that its heroine was called to life through the emotional investment of its players. Lara Croft, too, relies on an identificatory empathy enabling one to forget that Lara is "only" virtual, that she is nothing more than pixel porridge. Granted virtual life in this way, Lara could step out of the screen and assume the status of universal medium and star, one who is loved and loves in return. And because her body is at once immaterial and *immortal,* she could be all the more certain of her fans' admiration. This ability to represent "life" forms the heart of her virtual stardom, a stardom quite different from that of Heidi or Enid Coleslaw.

Of course, Lara Croft no more possesses a real body than Heidi does. She lacks the physical quality that gives life to cinematic images. In lending Lara Croft her body, Jolie allowed Lara to assume physical form. Yet contrary to all the concerns of her friends and agents, Jolie's part in the *Tomb Raider* movie did nothing to harm her career. Lara Croft is not just any video game character; she is a virtual star, one who, without exaggeration, helped make Jolie into a real one.

The Question of Sexual Difference

L et me recapitulate the arguments I have presented. We have seen how the multiple origins of Lara's success contained overlapping mechanisms determined by economic, medial, and sexual structures. Together these mechanisms formed a dynamic in which the phenomenon of Lara Croft became an imaginary illusion, a fusion and identification with a decentered image. We also saw that the media fever surrounding Lara Croft was no peripheral phenomenon but an integral part of this very dynamic. Outside the game, Lara Croft acted as a kind of adhesive holding together separate media in a single media society. Even Lara's becoming real through the bodies of her models functioned as a *medial* event. Finally I showed how Lara Croft's incarnation blurred the line between reality and virtuality while leaving the distinction between a *true* and a *false* reality intact. Because the ideality of the virtual woman was elevated to true reality, Lara Croft not only appeared faster, more beautiful, more perfect, but also promised to fulfill men's and women's fantasies of power. As a universal reference system for desire, the phenomenon of Lara Croft drew her "life" from the phantasm of a fulfilled reality.

Now, all this might not have been a problem if the phenomenon of Lara Croft did not, as we have also seen, devalue the everyday reality in which we structure our lives: the reality we share with others just as imperfect as ourselves; the reality in which we eat, sleep, wake, dress, and work; the reality in which we are young and grow old; the reality in which we form and break relationships; the reality in which we ultimately die.

This devaluation reveals itself quite overtly in the relationship between Lara Croft and her models. Violently reduced to a body whose value must remain temporary, a single model, any one female body, is not enough to incarnate immortal Lara. It is a relationship that seems to resurrect the concept of the "king's two bodies," the medieval legal fiction according to which kings incorporated the unity and perpetuity of the kingdom through a strange doubling of their mortal bodies. Ernst H. Kantorowicz has documented how the corporatist view of kingship developed out of the theological doctrine of Christ's two natures, ultimately giving rise to the secular state personified by the king as sovereign. To establish the immortality of the king's body politic over and beyond the death of his natural body, the former—the king's so-called dignity—was symbolized by an effigy. With the funeral of Edward II in 1327, the custom began of placing a "roiall representation" on top of the king's coffin. The effigy was

> made of wood or of leather padded with bombast and covered with plaster . . . [and] dressed in the coronation garments or, later on, in the parliamentary robe. . . . [It] displayed the insignia of sovereignty: on the head of the

> image (worked apparently since Henry VII after the
> death mask) there was the crown, while the artificial
> hands held orb and scepter.[1]

Even if sixteenth-century France went so far as to serve, feed, wash, and care for the royal representation, the immortality it established—that "decisive mark" of the king's divinity achieved through a "proud reconquest of a terrestrial *aevum*"—was always in danger of losing its "absolute, or even its imaginary values."[2] The death of a mortal king brought with it the demand for an immediate, living substitute, as reflected in the cry "The king is dead! Long live the king!" Kantorowicz writes, "Unless [immortality] manifested itself incessantly through new mortal incarnations, it practically ceased to be immortality."[3] Without a mortal body, the royal representations lost more than their immortality. Without a mortal body, they became merely dead machines.

Just as the royal representation drew its immortal life from the mortal bodies of the kings, so Lara Croft draws her reality from the bodies of her models. Yet unlike the kings, whose mortal bodies could at least represent their political ones for an earthly lifetime, the reign of Lara Croft's real-life models was reduced to a year. Does this have to do with the fact that Lara Croft's kingdom is not of this world, that her kingdom is emphatically nonpolitical?

True, a "Lara Croft for President" campaign may once have circulated through the media, but the more important question raised by her "nomination" is, Who possesses the *real* power, our political leaders or the media?

While Lara does not represent a political community, she does represent a media community, one whose members are not citizens but users. The establishment of this community requires neither elections nor decisions. It requires only that the machines keep moving, that they, in other words, remain (virtually) alive. The community's human members become, as McLuhan put it, "the sex organ of the machine world, as the bee of the plant world, enabling it to fecundate and to evolve ever new forms."[4]

Lara Croft does not represent political power, as the immortal bodies of the kings once did, but represents the desire for power itself. If, as Ward remarked, "the boys" invest their sexual interest in Lara, they do so because playing *Tomb Raider* delivers a higher degree of narcissistic fulfillment than the pursuit of pleasure with another. Female fans are attracted to Lara for the same reason. Part of what constitutes Lara's independence is the absence of relationships to others. Sexy as she is, Lara has no sex life, neither in the game nor in the life invented for her by Eidos.

Lara's origins have shown that she is not female by chance but, as woman, the source of the desire to represent and the medium through which desire is objectified. She is, as de Lauretis wrote, both ground of representation and representation itself. Once again: the dream woman is a construct, a fiction, a speculation, one that nevertheless arouses desire and promises more—more sex, more body, more life—than the multiplicity of women. The reality that the dream woman is "only" a virtual figure does nothing to change this. That is why all those who argue that the supernatural size of Lara's breasts makes them unrealistic miss the point. Her oversize feminine attributes are not supposed to distinguish her as a "natural" woman, a mortal woman among many. Quite the contrary: her breasts are meant to convey that she is a body in a very speculative and abstract sense. Lara can neither suffer pain nor feel desire. She is a supernatural "body," a body in the way that the Cosmic Matrix, the mother of God, and the Primal Mother are bodies: immortal, virgin, never ending.

That Lara Croft makes an appearance in the fifth installment of *Tomb Raider* wearing the same outfit as the character Trinity from the Hollywood film *The Matrix* (1999) speaks volumes for the otherworldliness of her body. It not only shows the subtle ways in which messages are transmitted through images; it also makes clear that these loaded images are exceptionally powerful, especially when they are not "read" but perceived solely on their own, on the level of the imaginary. As in the case of *The Matrix*, such images are usually citations from the cultural stock of religious—primarily Christian—symbolism. Using the template and characters of a Christian tale of redemption, *The Matrix* is about a search for true reality that ends in a fight to free the world, a showdown that would have done any Western proud. Trinity—the redeemer of the redeemer—is a mixture of the Virgin Mary and Joan of Arc. Such allusions, of which there are countless others, are transferred to Lara Croft via Trinity's black, skintight suit. The suit becomes an emblem in which Lara Croft is clothed, one that carries the same messages and meanings as *The Matrix*'s heroine.

Lara's unnatural body dimensions, her supernatural body, thus promise what the "mind" and data structures alone cannot: immediacy, fulfillment, materiality. These abstract notions are given a supposed concrete existence through their representation in the female body. Lara Croft thus reproduces the equation "woman = body." She stands for the reduction of women to their bodies.

How does this reduction relate to the shift of meaning

currently taking place in the concepts of sex and gender? The identification of woman and body is just as old as the splitting of body and mind. It continues Descartes' well-known dualism where body stands for spatial extension (*res intensa*) and mind for thought (*res cognitas*). What is new, however, is the radicality with which biologically based conceptions of sexual difference have dissociated from the sexual body and become independent entities. This radicality is an effect of the "second computer revolution," an effect, that is to say, of the technology that allows virtual realities to be experienced through the senses. If, as McLuhan claimed, film made configurations on-screen appear organic, then the computer—whether PC or game console— made interaction with virtual figures possible. By clothing abstract concepts in images,[5] the technology of virtual worlds also enabled interaction with the dream woman, the one de Lauretis so aptly described as a speculation. By identifying Lara's female attributes with the immortal body, the metaphysics of gender implicit in this technology project the phantasm of a fulfilled reality onto the virtual world. For her fans, Lara Croft's female form, that abstract reference system of desire, seems more human than humans; the dream woman seems more woman than women. The new media use technological means to cement the dualistic order of the sexes on an abstract level. This return to a metaphysics of gender runs parallel to the establishment of virtual reality as imaginary illusion.

Yet is this necessarily so? Must it be this way? Do the media not also open up new chances? Do theorists like Donna Haraway, Allucquère Rosanne Stone, the so-called cyberfeminists, and the Old Boys Network not hold out the hope of overcoming the traditional order of the sexes with the help of new technologies?[6] On what are their hopes based? How do they argue? Take, for instance, Allucquère Rosanne Stone. She makes a basic distinction between two possible positions vis-à-vis the computer. For those who take the first view, the computer will appear as a machine like the telephone, one that is basically the same as traditional media. For those who take the second, computers become arenas for social experiments and dramatic interactions. The computer becomes more like a medium such as theater. The interaction occurs not between user and reference system of desire but between multiple individuals communicating with one another.

Stone makes quite clear that the question is not which of the positions is closer to the computer's "essence," which, that is, is "truer."[7] Rather, certain conditions must first be met before the second position can be actualized at all. According to Stone, the conditions depend not on the computer but on us. We must reflect on our notions of immediacy, of presence, in order to turn virtual worlds into a kind of theater, to use them as a field of social experimentation. Of course, reflecting on presence also means reflecting on what is meant by "being a body" in the new media. The question is closely tied with the ability to act. If, as the phenomenon of Lara Croft has shown, the imaginary illusion goes hand in hand with a loss of surface and distance, then achieving distance is the first step toward being able to act, the first step toward finding a body concept that doesn't fall prey to the phantasm of a fulfilled reality. As we have seen, Žižek follows Lacan in making the case for the recovery of a "blind spot." Having one or not marks the difference between seeing *something* and seeing *nothing at all.* The recovery of a blind spot is about—and this cannot be emphasized enough—a recovery of *appearances,* not of truth. This is what Žižek means when he contrasts the imaginary illusion with the symbolic fiction.

This blind spot is so important because it guarantees an opening that prevents the disturbing part of virtual reality from being satisfied in a closed narcissistic cycle. By pleading for a blind spot, Žižek insists on knowing what the awareness of not knowing presupposes. This is precisely where sexual difference comes into play.

Following the leads of Judith Butler and Geneviève Fraisse, I have suggested that sexual difference be understood as an irresolvable question, a place of unrest situated at the limits of knowledge, and which interrogates their foundations. More palpably than Žižek's blind spot, the question of sexual difference revolves around the separation of culture and nature; it revolves around the relationship between this separation and the distinction between body and mind; and it revolves around the question of how these oppositions relate to the metaphysics of gender. We have seen how Lara Croft has been erected as a kind of fetish at the site where the unrest of sexual difference would otherwise be situated. Indeed, one might say that Lara functions as a kind of *apotropaeum,* a magic potion to avert harm. It is no accident that her first name recalls the Lares, those ancient Roman spirits protecting house and family; nor does it come as a surprise that her last name means bordered field or property.[8] Like the figure itself, Lara's name conjures up the spirits that guard hearth and home, the *Heimliche,* and the idyll from the onset of the Real. The virtual woman is a fetish whose function is to deny the gap opening before the indecidability of nature and culture and to immunize thought against the onset of historicity. The question of sexual difference, in contrast, confronts us with both, with indecidability and historicity. In its irresolvability it calls on us to interrogate the opposition of culture and nature always anew. It subverts every attempt to pin down what a woman, what a man, what a body is. It undermines every answer by qualifying it as preliminary. The question of sexual difference becomes an antidote to narcissistic identification and the metaphysics of gender.

Stone thinks the computer can be a kind of theater; Teresa de Lauretis proposes that we "perform" the terms that generate woman as text. Both approaches allow the body to appear in a new way: as a chance to experience. That this is also possible in the case of Lara Croft was demonstrated by several participants at the International Women's University in Hanover during the summer of 2000. Their "Kidnapping Lara Action" involved seizing a life-size Lara Croft figure from a computer store, clothing her in dress from various different cultures, and placing her in everyday situations (such as the bathroom). After the event, photos of the dressed-up Lara were posted on the Internet and presented from the perspectives of modern and postmodern feminist criticism.[9] Before returning the cardboard Lara to the computer store, the women affixed to it hundreds of paper strips, each noting the URL of some Web-based feminist initiative. Summing up their experience in a sentence, the women wrote: "We enjoyed experimenting with Lara as well as with possible meanings that differed from those offered by media and industry."

13

Afterplay: The Next Generation

Of the one thousand words said by the name Lara, one is "immortality." Yet even an immortal Lara Croft has quickly grown old in a video game market whose fast-moving nature stands in irresolvable conflict with longevity. One clear indication of Lara's aging process has been her models. They began getting younger just as *Tomb Raider*'s decline began to seem inevitable.

The turn in the game's popularity started when retail sales of the fourth episode did not reach those projected by the success of *Tomb Raider III*. The reason lay in the rapid development of hardware technology and compatible game software. The 3-D technology that allowed Toby Gard to dream of developing a real-time interactive movie in 1996 had soon become an industry standard. Moreover, *Tomb Raider*'s complete reliance on its original 3-D design did not allow for genuine structural or conceptual innovations. For all its new versions, the game never really changed: whether diving, climbing, jumping, somersaulting, fighting, or shooting, it was always the same old Lara. *Tomb Raider*'s ability to capture the attention of the "video-playing nation" outside the die-hard fan community began to wane,[1] especially as the Lara of the game lost more and more ground to the Lara of advertising. As a result, *Tomb Raider* began to receive bad press from leading game magazines.

While fans were worrying about Lara's future, developers at Core Design had already started work on a new game concept, one designed to exploit the new technical capabilities of the next generation of game platforms and present them in the familiar *Tomb Raider* format. The 128-bit platform found its first manifestation in Sony's PlayStation 2. Its release in 2000 aroused a flood of media hype. Unlike advancements with past consoles, the most important improvement in the PlayStation 2 was not picture quality but multimedia capability. The PlayStation 2 was equipped with an integrated DVD player and ports for Internet and broadband network connections. In addition to video games, the console could also play DVD movies and audio CDs. Another new-generation platform, the Xbox from Microsoft, was given an Ethernet interface for online gaming. Through the use of radio chips, the new consoles could even transfer data via cell phone. Conceived as "multimedia entertainment centers," these platforms were designed to be compatible with existing and emerging technologies.[2]

Lara Croft's success and history were closely tied to the older generation of hardware, yet developers at Core Design knew that her future depended on the ability to adapt to the new platforms. As a precaution, they made Lara die a symbolic death so that they could resurrect her again in new form on the next generation of systems. *Tomb Raider IV*, tellingly subtitled "The Last Revelation," ends with Lara's apparent demise under the rubble of a collapsed Egyptian pyramid. The next chapter in the series, released in late November 2000, prepares players for

Lara's return even as it continues the story of her death. "Chronicles" begins with a memorial service for the heroine in the Croft Manor garden. Afterward Lara's friends gather inside and reveal that Lara is only missing, that she may not be dead after all. The friends recall some of the relic hunter's past, as yet-untold adventures, which the player then lives out one by one. In the last adventure, Lara appears in the *Matrix* suit mentioned in the last chapter, giving players a glimpse of the transformation to come.

In a September 2000 interview, Adrian Smith, Core Design's then operating director, was asked whether Lara was really dead. His reply stressed the role of hardware development in the decision to end the fourth episode the way it does:

> The important thing with *Tomb Raider* was finishing the franchise as we know it and on PlayStation at a point that allowed us to have a clean start. That's why we came up with the idea of leaving Lara locked up in an Egyptian pyramid. It allows us not to take any of the baggage over from *Tomb Raider*.[3]

Later in the interview, Smith revealed that the next generation of *Tomb Raider* was to be designed specifically with the new technology in mind. It was also to concentrate more on the Lara Croft figure than the original series had.

Because the new consoles were meant not as a children's rec room toy but as a central multimedia junction connecting household occupants with streams of input/output data, Core Design developers conceived the new game for a significantly older audience. One picture that appeared on the Internet gave a taste of what they had in mind. It showed a masked man in a black leather bodysuit, chained and hanging on a cross. Informing this image were the movies from which the new game was supposed to take its cue. Smith remarks, "We've looked at films like *The Omen* and *The Exorcist,* which are very dark and deep kind of films, and that gives some kind of indication of what you can expect to see."[4] According to Smith, the next-generation Lara is a person who might become an alcoholic or start taking drugs, someone who leads a very different life than the Lara of before.

The new content included plans for a corresponding change in form. Instead of a single one-and-out adventure like the games from the first series, the new game was to be made up of weekly episodes to be downloaded from the Internet. Each episode was to be self-contained but connected to the others through a larger story line, just as with the popular television show *The X-Files.* At an Eidos promotional party in 2002, Smith called the story line of the new *Tomb Raider* "epic," the same word that Sony used to describe the PlayStation 2 when it was released in 2000. Sony, too, spoke of PlayStation 2 games that would continue each week like TV soap operas. New installments would no longer be available in retail stores but would be offered directly on the Internet, where the player could pay via credit card or direct debit.

But rather than moving the consoles toward multiuser networks, the technical imagination behind new-generation platforms confined itself to creating a virtual distribution system complete with one-way communication and bank-account access. The wholesale commercialization of software development was not a recipe for success. Instead games became more and more alike, and developers failed to realize the potential of the new medium.

Particularly disastrous for *Tomb Raider* was Core's decision to impose a predetermined idea of what constituted the game of the future. *Angel of Darkness,* the anxiously awaited "next-gen" game, was a great disappointment. After many delays, *Angel of Darkness* was rushed onto the market in summer 2003. Besides its technical imperfections and bugs, the game didn't fulfill the hopes of Smith's vision. *Angel of Darkness* was no revolutionary epic; it was merely a new addition to the old series.

The one-sided concern with economics brought with it a high price. Core's founder and managing director Jeremy Heath-Smith took the blame for the game's poor performance and stepped down from the boards of Core and Eidos. Two weeks after Heath-Smith's resignation, Eidos terminated Core's relationship with the *Tomb Raider* franchise. Lara Croft's future currently rests in the hands of the California-based software developer Crystal Dynamics. The next Lara Croft game is scheduled to be released in 2005.

Will the virtual figure ever regain the brilliant success she once had? Only if, one conjectures, she can proclaim the message of the new technology with as much credibility as she did for the older generation.

And the women? Can Lara succeed again in winning them over? At this point, it's up for grabs.

Notes

1. The Phenomenon of Lara Croft

1. Lara Croft's Official Homepage, "Letters to Lara."

2. I would like to thank Roman for helping me with many questions, as well as for patiently introducing me to the video game world. For their encouragement and critical comments, I would also like to thank Ursula Konnertz, Gabriele Dietze, Giaco Schiesser, and Wolf-Dieter Besche.

3. *Lara Croft Magazin,* no. 1 (1999): 27.

4. "License to Thrill."

5. Benson, "Lara Croft for President."

6. Arent, "Game Maker: Lara's No Playmate."

2. A Duplicitous Gift

1. Quoted in Vorsatz, "Bitte bleiben Sie dran." [Unless otherwise noted, all translations are my own.—Trans.]

2. Angela McRobbie remarks that Lara Croft's biography "is closer than we may like to think to the boarding school story." See McRobbie, "Coding the Feminine in the 1990s," 6.

3. Sherry Turkle has pointed out that the contemporary notion of "user" didn't appear until the late 1970s, when application programs

were first used to help operate personal computers. The programs allowed people to use the computer "without getting involved with the 'guts' of the machine" (*Life on the Screen*, 32–34). While Turkle welcomes the removal of the computer's inner mechanisms from the user's purview as a creation of new space on which to "float, skim, and play" (34), Friedrich Kittler has rightly warned against losing sight of the conditions determined by hardware market development. These conditions could "reduce the contingency or unpredictability of some, but not all, futures by finite degrees" ("Hardware, das unbekannte Wesen," 131).

4. Elsner et al., "Zur Kulturgeschichte der Medien," 163.

5. On the relationship between machine and medium and its history, see Schelhowe, *Das Medium aus der Maschine*.

6. Žižek, *The Plague of Fantasies*, 132.

7. On the consequences of this development and its critique, see Kittler, "Hardware, das unbekannte Wesen," 124.

8. Cf. Mainzer, *Computernetze und virtuelle Realität*, 22.

9. Marx, *Capital*, 115. Here Marx cites the passage from *Timon of Athens* where Timon, having just discovered gold, proclaims, "Come, damned earth, / Thou common whore of mankind." The reliance on sexual difference in Shakespeare's metaphorics is, as Walter Benjamin has shown, likewise no accident. See my "Woman: The Most Precious Loot in the 'Triumph of Allegory,'" 281–303.

10. Butler, "The End of Sexual Difference?" 414–34.

11. Fraisse, *Geschlecht und Moderne*, 28.

12. On Butler's critique of the distinction between sex and gender, see her *Gender Trouble*, 7; as well as my "Geschlecht als philosophische Kategorie," 11–31.

13. Stone, "Will the Real Bodies Please Stand Up?" 94.

14. Ibid.

3. The Origins of a Cultural Icon

1. *Lara Croft Magazin*, 7.

2. In the summer of 1999, the Krisztina de Châtel Dance Group performed the piece "Lara" at the Over Het IJ Festival. Commenting on

the work, the festival's coproducer Judith Huizing said, "We were fascinated by the story of Lara, that she's world-famous and doesn't even exist" ("Lara Comes to Life").

3. Quoted in Poole, *Trigger Happy*, 8.

4. The Market and the Hardware

1. Heath-Smith, "Sie kämpft mit Wölfen," 23.

2. Ibid.

3. See Langer, "Mythos Lara Croft," 91.

5. Medial Origins and Sexual Grounds

1. McLuhan, *Understanding Media*, 284.

2. Ibid., 57.

3. Ibid., 8.

4. Ibid.

5. Heath-Smith, "Sie kämpft mit Wölfen," 24. George Lucas produced the Indiana Jones trilogy.

6. Ibid.

7. Quoted in Gibbon, "Q&A: The Man Who Made Lara."

8. See Lara's Homepage.

9. Calvino, *Invisible Cities*, 52.

10. De Lauretis, *Alice Doesn't*, 13.

11. Ibid., 5.

12. See my "Geschlecht und Repräsentation," 24–42.

13. Ibid., 36.

14. Haraway, *Primate Visions*, 139. For more on the history of the term "cyborg" and its intersection with that of "automaton," see Bredekamp, "Zur Unausweichlichkeit der Automaten," 102.

15. For a more detailed account of Lara's creation, see Poole, "Lara's Story."

16. Gunzenhäuser, "Womb Raider," 60.

17. Mike Ward has observed that while the Lara Croft of the video game, who can be seen only from behind, offers herself to the gaze of the player, the real-life model embodying Lara looks down over her

sunglasses at the camera (Ward, "Being Lara Croft"). In chapter 7, I will take up Ward's interesting analysis of gaze and desire in more detail.

6. Virtual Reality

1. McLuhan, *Understanding Media*, 284.

2. Ibid., 284–85.

3. Ibid., 12.

4. Ibid.

5. Cf. Kittler, "Romantik—Psychoanlyse—Film," 81–104.

6. McLuhan, *Understanding Media*, 12. In her cleverly titled essay "Das ein-gebildete Geschlecht," Christina von Braun examines the traditions that ground this imaginary return to the image and considers its consequences for thinking about sexual difference (149–70).

7. Krämer, "Zentralperspektive, Kalkül, Virtuelle Realität," 32.

8. Ibid., 33.

9. See Eco, "Mirrors," in *Semiotics and the Philosophy of Language,* 216.

10. Krämer, "Zentralperspektive, Kalkül, Virtuelle Realität," 33.

11. Ibid.

12. Ibid.

13. Esposito, "Fiktion und Virtualität," 269.

14. Poole, *Trigger Happy,* 133.

15. See Clark, "Rear-View Mirrorshades," 115.

7. The Interactive Movie

1. The CAVE (Cave Automatic Virtual Environment) is a "surround screen" and "surround sound" room for projecting immersion in a 3-D world. By wearing special glasses and gloves, CAVE users can "move" in virtual spaces and "touch" computer-generated objects.

2. Ward, "Being Lara Croft."

3. Ibid.

4. Poole, *Trigger Happy,* 133. Although Poole emphasizes that no game comes as close to cinema as *Tomb Raider,* he remains silent as to the ramifications. Unlike Mike Ward, Poole ignores the structural

importance of sexual difference for the cinematic apparatus, considering neither *Tomb Raider*'s film-based medial logic nor the specific character of the interactive movie (65).

5. See my "Geschlecht und Repräsentation," 33.

6. Mulvey, "Visual Pleasure and Narrative Cinema," 28–40.

7. Lacan, *Écrits: A Selection*, 1–8.

8. Freud, "Fetishism," 157.

9. *Heise Online*, reader commentary to Thomas Willman's article "Give Me PlayStation or Death [sic]." [The German *Schwanz* usually means "tail" but is also slang for "cock." In the dialogue, the author assumes the reader will recognize the double meaning of *Pferdeschwanz* (ponytail).—Trans.]

10. Cyberstar, "Star Portraits."

11. "Interview with Lara Croft," *Croft Times*, June 5, 1997.

12. See Doane, "Film and the Masquerade," 41–57. Doane responds to a question implicitly posed in Mulvey's analysis but ultimately left unanswered: if woman represents the cinematic image, how should we understand the (impossible) position of the woman spectator and her own voyeurism? Doane's responses to this question have triggered a wide range of discussion and alternative concepts. Cf. de Lauretis, *The Practice of Love*.

13. McRobbie, "Coding the Feminine in the 1990s," 6.

14. Gunzenhäuser, "Womb Raider," 56.

15. Ibid., 57.

16. Ibid., 59.

8. The Loss of Surface

1. Žižek, *The Plague of Fantasies*, 134.

2. [This passage was added to the *The Plague of Fantasies* for the German edition, which the author cites. See *Die Pest der Phantasmen: Die Effizienz des Phantasmatischen in den neuen Medien*, trans. Leopold Andreas Hofbauer (Vienna: Passagen Verlag, 1997), 94.—Trans.]

3. In this connection, Žižek criticizes Turkle and others for idealizing the postmodern attitude of tinkering. To maintain this valuation of

the postmodern, Žižek writes, the facticity of the concrete life-world [*Lebenswelt*] existing outside cyberspace must be abandoned. Postmodernists like Turkle fail to notice that their "non-transparent life-world already presupposes a background of the scientific digital universe" (*The Plague of Fantasies*, 132). Mike Sandbothe goes in a similar direction when he criticizes Turkle for presupposing a "media-neutral" perspective in her analysis, thereby overlooking the fact that "RL identity is already influenced by the use of other media (such as printing or television)." See Sandbothe, "Transversale Medienwelten," 63.

4. Žižek, *The Plague of Fantasies*, 132.

5. Ward, "Being Lara Croft."

6. The ability to act critically and the precondition for a critical theory of media and gender studies also depend on this distinction. I understand "critique" in the broad sense understood by Michel Foucault as "the art of not being governed or, better, the art of not being governed like that and at that cost" ("What Is Critique?" 29).

7. Žižek, *The Plague of Fantasies*, 136. Žižek criticizes Judith Butler's attempt to oppose the "natural phallus" with the "lesbian phallus," a term she introduces in *Bodies That Matter* in order to denaturalize Lacan's sense of the term. What Žižek points out, however, is that Lacan's concept of the phallus is itself ambiguous. As a signifier, the phallus "'as such' *is* a kind of 'prosthetic,' 'artificial,' supplement" (ibid.). Whether the phallus represents an imaginary illusion or a symbolic fiction depends solely on the stance that a given individual takes to it. Incidentally, Žižek's critique does not apply to "The End of Sexual Difference?" the essay from Butler I refer to elsewhere. For more on Žižek's argument, see my "Geschlecht als philosophische Kategorie," 12.

8. Žižek, *The Plague of Fantasies*, 136.

9. Imaginary closure finds an equivalent in McLuhan's expression "sense closure" (*Understanding Media*, 45–46).

10. Ibid., 133.

11. Cf. Angerer, *Body Options*.

12. Butler, "The End of Sexual Difference?" 416–17.

13. Ibid., 417.

9. The Medialization of the Body

1. Quoted in Polsky, "Skins, Patches, and Plug-ins."

2. Fans could even watch the event on the Internet the following day. See "Lara in Platin."

3. Before the release of *Tomb Raider II,* a group of musicians including Yello and Depeche Mode recorded the album *A Tribute to Lara Croft.* Later the German band Die Ärzte shot a music video with Lara Croft, helping them to their first number one hit. See "Lara on Stage," *Lara Croft Magazin,* 95–97.

4. Langer, "Mythos Lara Croft," 88.

10. The Universal Medium

1. Sandbothe, "Transversale Medienwelten," 73.

2. As his examples demonstrate, Sandbothe understands the "real" not as the programmed machine command—the correct definition of the real in this case—but as a connection to another symbol that remains on the surface. This imprecise use of the term "real" is symptomatic of the increasingly common tendency to conflate surface with reality.

3. Cf. Tombraiders, "Lara Croft: Feminist Media Critique and Audience Response." The author stresses that content analysis, semiotics, and psychoanalysis all "have their limitations in analyzing a multi-faceted, multi-reality, and multi-identity pop icon such as Lara Croft."

4. McLuhan, *Understanding Media,* 22.

5. Ibid., 31.

6. Ibid.

7. See "Female Sunglasses Wearer of the Year."

11. *Tomb Raider:* The Movie

1. "Review of Lara Croft: Tomb Raider," *Croft Times.*

2. Roger Ebert, review of *Lara Croft: Tomb Raider.*

3. Huschke, "Amazone auf Acid," 49.

4. Angelina Jolie, interview by Paul Semel.

5. The history of Heidi as a medium is well documented in Halter,

Heidi: Karrieren einer Figur. See also the official home page of the exhibition commemorating the one hundredth anniversary of Johanna Spyri's death, Heidi: Mythos—Marke—Medienstar, http://www.heidi01.ch/.

6. See, for instance, MGM's *Ghost World* site, http://www.mgm.com/ghostworld/ie/index.html.

7. See Butler, *Star Texts.*

12. The Question of Sexual Difference

1. Kantorowicz, *The King's Two Bodies,* 420–21.

2. Ibid., 436–37.

3. Ibid., 437.

4. McLuhan, *Understanding Media,* 46.

5. Even Immanuel Kant speaks of rational concepts that "normally assume, so to speak, a corporeal cloak" (Kant, "Dreams of a Spirit-Seer Elucidated by Dreams of Metaphysics," 326).

6. See Old Boys Network, http://www.obn.org/.

7. Stone, *Desire and Technology at the Close of the Mechanical Age,* 16.

8. I would like to thank Giaco Schiesser for pointing out the etymology of Lara Croft's name.

9. Web site of the International Women's University, "Lara Croft and Feminism," August 2000, http://www.vifu.de/students/gendering/lara/home.html.

13. Afterplay

1. See Emmerling, "Tomb Raider: Die Chronik," 79.

2. In advertisements, Microsoft refers to its Xbox console as the "multimedia entertainment center for the next generation." See also *GameStar,* 124.

3. Smith, "Tomb Raider Next Generation."

4. Ibid.

Bibliography

Angerer, Marie-Luise. *Body Options: Körper, Spuren, Medien, Bilder.* Vienna: Turia and Kant, 2000.

Arent, Lindsey. "Game Maker: Lara's No Playmate." *Wired News,* July 15, 1999. http://www.wired.com/news/culture/0,1284,20762,00.html.

Benson, Lynn. "Lara Croft for President." *Rightgrrl!* October 30, 1998. http://www.rightgrrl.com/1998/laracroft.html.

Braun, Christina von. "Das ein-gebildete Geschlecht: Bilderverbot, Bilderverehrung und Geschlechterbilder." In *Der Zweite Blick: Bildgeschichte und Bildreflexion,* ed. Hans Belting and Dietmar Kamper. Munich: Wilhelm Fink, 2000.

Bredekamp, Horst. "Zur Unausweichlichkeit der Automaten." In *Puppen, Körper, Automaten: Phantasmen der Moderne,* ed. Pia Müller-Tamm and Katharina Sykora. Cologne: Oktagon, 1999.

Butler, Jeremy G., ed. *Star Texts: Image and Performance in Film and Television.* Contemporary Film and Television Series. Detroit: Wayne State University Press, 1991.

Butler, Judith. *Gender Trouble: Feminism and the Subversion of Identity.* New York: Routledge, 1990.

———. *Bodies That Matter: On the Discursive Limits of "Sex."* New York: Routledge, 1993.

———. "The End of Sexual Difference?" In *Feminist Consequences: Theory for the New Century,* ed. Elisabeth Bronfen and Misha Kavka. New York: Columbia University Press, 2001.

Calvino, Italo. *Invisible Cities.* Trans. William Weaver. New York: Harcourt Brace Jovanovich, 1974.

Clark, Nigel. "Rear-View Mirrorshades: The Recursive Generation of the Cyberbody." In *Cyberspace, Cyberbodies, Cyberpunk: Cultures of Technological Embodiment,* ed. Mike Featherstone and Roger Burrows. London: Sage, 1995.

Cyberstar. "Star Portraits." http://www.cyberstar.de (accessed July 7, 1999; site now discontinued).

de Lauretis, Teresa. *Alice Doesn't: Feminism, Semiotics, Cinema.* Bloomington: Indiana University Press, 1984.

———. *The Practice of Love: Lesbian Sexuality and Perverse Desire.* Bloomington: Indiana University Press, 1994.

Deuber-Mankowsky, Astrid. "Geschlecht und Repräsentation: Oder wie das Bild zum Denken kommt." *Die Philosophin* 18 (1998).

———. "Woman: The Most Precious Loot in the 'Triumph of Allegory': On the Function and Appearance of Gender Relations in Walter Benjamin's *Passagenwerk.*" Trans. Dana Hollander. In *Continental Philosophy in Feminist Perspective: Re-reading the Canon in German,* ed. Herta Nagl-Docekal and Cornelia Klinger. University Park: Penn State University Press, 2000.

———. "Geschlecht als philosophische Kategorie." *Die Philosophin* 23 (2001).

Doane, Mary Ann. "Film and the Masquerade: Theorizing the Female Spectator." In *Issues in Feminist Film Criticism,* ed. Patricia Erens. Bloomington: Indiana University Press, 1990.

Ebert, Roger. Review of *Lara Croft: Tomb Raider. Chicago Sun-Times,* June 15, 2001.

Eco, Umberto. *Semiotics and the Philosophy of Language.* London: Macmillan, 1984.

Elsner, Monika, et al. "Zur Kulturgeschichte der Medien." In *Die Wirklichkeit der Medien: Eine Einführung in die Kommunikationswissenschaft,* ed. Klaus Merten, Siegfried J. Schmidt, and Siegfried Wischenberg. Opladen: Westdeutscher Verlag, 1994.

Emmerling, Frank. "Tomb Raider: Die Chronik." *PlayStation: Das offizielle Playstation-Magazin*, no. 1 (2001).

Esposito, Elena. "Fiktion und Virtualität." In *Medien, Computer, Realität*, ed. Sybille Krämer. Frankfurt am Main: Suhrkamp, 1998.

"Female Sunglasses Wearer of the Year." *Croft Times*, April 9, 2000. http://www.cubeit.com/ctimes/news/2000/04/news0586.html.

Foucault, Michel. "What Is Critique?" Trans. Lysa Hochroth. In *The Politics of Truth*, ed. Sylvère Lotringer and Lysa Hochroth. New York: Semiotext(e), 1997.

Fraisse, Geneviève. *Geschlecht und Moderne: Archäologien der Gleichberechtigung*. Ed. Eva Horn. Frankfurt am Main: Fischer Taschenbuch Verlag, 1995.

Freud, Sigmund. "Fetishism" (1927). In *The Standard Edition of the Complete Psychological Works of Sigmund Freud*, ed. and trans. James E. Strachey, vol. 21. London: Hogarth Press, 1961.

"Game Consoles." Special issue, *GameStar*, no. 1 (2001).

Gibbon, David. "Q&A: The Man Who Made Lara." Interview with Toby Gard. *BBC Online*, June 28, 2001. http://news.bbc.co.uk/1/hi/entertainment/new_media/1410480.stm.

Gunzenhäuser, Randi. "Womb Raider." Interview with Randi Gunzenhäuser. Trans. John Brogden. In *LaraCroftism*, ed. Manuela Barth. Munich: Kunstraum München, 1999.

Halter, Ernst, ed. *Heidi: Karrieren einer Figur*. Zurich: Offizin Verlag, 2001.

Haraway, Donna. *Primate Visions: Gender, Race, and Nature in the World of Modern Science*. New York: Routledge, 1990.

Heath-Smith, Jeremy. "Sie kämpft mit Wölfen." Interview with Jeremy Heath-Smith. *Lara Croft Magazin*, no. 1 (1999).

Heise Online. Telepolis. Reader commentary to Thomas Willman's article "Give Me PlaySation or Death [*sic*]," November 24, 2000. http://www.heise.de/tp/foren/go.shtml?read=1&msg_id=767635&forum_id=14891&showthread=1.

Huschke, Roland. "Amazone auf Acid." Review of *Lara Croft: Tomb Raider. Tip,* no. 13 (July 2001).

"Interview with Lara Croft." *Croft Times,* June 5, 1997. http://www.cubeit.com/ctimes/press03.htm.

Jolie, Angelina. Interview by Paul Semel. *GameSpyDaily,* June 5, 2001. http://www.gamespydaily.com/news/fullstory.asp?id=1907.

Kant, Immanuel. "Dreams of a Spirit-Seer Elucidated by Dreams of Metaphysics" (1766). In *Theoretical Philosophy, 1755–1770,* ed. David Walford. Cambridge Edition of the Works of Immanuel Kant. Cambridge: Cambridge University Press, 2003.

Kantorowicz, Ernst H. *The King's Two Bodies: A Study in Mediaeval Political Theology.* Princeton: Princeton University Press, 1957.

Kittler, Friedrich. "Romantik—Psychoanalyse—Film: Eine Doppelgängergeschichte." In *Draculas Vermächtnis: Technische Schriften.* Dresden: Reclam, 1993.

———. "Hardware, das unbekannte Wesen." In *Medien, Computer, Realität: Wirklichkeitsvorstellungen und Neue Medien,* ed. Sybille Krämer. Frankfurt am Main: Suhrkamp, 1998.

Krämer, Sybille. "Zentralperspektive, Kalkül, Virtuelle Realität." In *Medien-Welten Wirklichkeiten,* ed. Gianni Vattimo and Wolfgang Welsch. Munich: Wilhelm Fink, 1998.

Lacan, Jacques. *Écrits: A Selection.* Trans. Alan Sheridan. 1977. Reprint, New York: Routledge, 2002.

Langer, Jörg. "Mythos Lara Croft." *GameStar,* no. 1 (1999).

"Lara Comes to Life." *Wired News,* June 25, 1999. http://www.wired.com/news/culture/0,1284,20406,00.html.

Lara Croft's Official Homepage. "Letters to Lara." http://www.laracroft.co.uk/letters/letter1.html (accessed October 18, 2000; site now discontinued).

"Lara in Platin." *Croft Times* [German edition], February 20, 2000. http://www.croft-times.de/cover139.htm.

"Lara on Stage." *Lara Croft Magazin,* no. 1 (1999).

Lara's Homepage. http://ww.nant.de/lar...me/thegame/index.shtml (accessed May 11, 1999; site now discontinued).

"License to Thrill." *BBC Online,* December 1, 1998. http://news.bbc
.co.uk/1/hi/sci/tech/225615.stm.

Mainzer, Klaus. *Computernetze und virtuelle Realität: Leben in der Wissensgesellschaft.* Berlin: Springer Verlag, 1999.

Marx, Karl. *Capital: A Critical Analysis of Capitalist Production.* London 1887. In *Gesamtausgabe,* by Karl Marx and Friedrich Engels, vol. 2.9, ed. Waltraud Falk et al. Berlin: Dietz Verlag, 1990.

McLuhan, Marshall. *Understanding Media: The Extensions of Man.* London: Routledge, 1994.

McRobbie, Angela. "Coding the Feminine in the 1990s." In *LaraCroftism,* ed. Manuela Barth. Munich: Kunstraum München, 1999.

Mulvey, Laura. "Visual Pleasure and Narrative Cinema." In *Issues in Feminist Film Criticism,* ed. Patricia Erens. Bloomington: Indiana University Press, 1990.

Polsky, Allyson D. "Skins, Patches, and Plug-ins: Becoming Woman in the New Gaming Culture." *Genders* 34 (2001). http://www.genders
.org/g34/g34_polsky.html.

Poole, Steven. *Trigger Happy: Videogames and the Entertainment Revolution.* New York: Arcade Publishing, 2000.

———. "Lara's Story." *The Guardian,* June 15, 2001. http://film
.guardian.co.uk/features/featurepages/0,4120,506934,00.html.

"Review of *Lara Croft: Tomb Raider.*" *Croft Times,* June 24, 2001. http://
www.cubeit.com/ctimes/news/2001/06/news0673.html.

Sandbothe, Mike. "Transversale Medienwelten." In *Medien-Welten Wirklichkeiten,* ed. Gianni Vattimo and Wolfgang Welsch. Munich: Wilhelm Fink, 1998.

Schelhowe, Heidi. *Das Medium aus der Maschine: Zur Metamorphose des Computers.* Frankfurt am Main: Campus Verlag, 1997.

Smith, Adrian. "Tomb Raider Next Generation." Interview with Adrian Smith. Originally appeared in *GameSpot,* September 2000, http://
gamespot.co.uk. Now available at http://pages.eidosnet.co.uk/
tombraid/croft-central/intervie.htm#ADRIAN SMITH.

Stone, Allucquère Rosanne. *Desire and Technology at the Close of the Mechanical Age.* Cambridge: MIT Press, 1995.

———. "Will the Real Bodies Please Stand Up? Boundary Stories about Virtual Cultures." In *Cybersexualities: A Reader on Feminist Theory, Cyborgs, and Cyberspace,* ed. Jenny Wolmark. Edinburgh: Edinburgh University Press, 2000.

Tombraiders. "Lara Croft: Feminist Media Critique and Audience Response." http://www.tombraiders.com/lara_croft/Essays/MissKris/default.htm (accessed March 27, 2000; site now discontinued).

Turkle, Sherry. *Life on the Screen: Identity in the Age of the Internet.* New York: Simon and Schuster, 1995.

Vorsatz, Marc. "Bitte bleiben Sie dran: Cyber-Heldin Lara Croft bringt die Werbung in die PC-Spiele." *Tagesspiegel,* April 14, 1999.

Ward, Mike. "Being Lara Croft, or We Are All Sci Fi." *PopMatters,* January 14, 2000. http://www.popmatters.com/features/000114-ward.html.

Žižek, Slavoj. *The Plague of Fantasies.* London: Verso, 1997.

Index

Astrid Deuber•Mankowsky is professor of media studies at Ruhr University Bochum, Germany, and cofounder and editor of *Die Philosophin*, a German journal on feminist theory and philosophy.

Dominic J. Bonfiglio is a freelance translator and a graduate student in philosophy at Humboldt University, Berlin.

Sue•Ellen Case is professor and chair of the critical studies program in the theater department at the University of California, Los Angeles. She is author of *The Domain Matrix: Performing Lesbian at the End of Print Culture* and editor of *Split Britches: Lesbian Practice/Feminist Performance.*

Electronic Mediations

Katherine Hayles, Mark Poster, and Samuel Weber
SERIES EDITORS